3 skeins or less

FRESH
knitted
accessories

Tanis Gray

INTERWEAVE
interweave

Editor Erica Smith

Technical Editor Alexandra Virgiel

Photographer Joe Hancock

Hair and Makeup Jen Murphy

Art Directors Julia Boyles & Charlene Tiedemann

Cover and Interior Design Brenda Gallagher

Production Kerry Jackson

Interweave
A division of F+W Media, Inc.
4868 Innovation Dr.
Fort Collins, CO 80525
interweave.com

Manufactured in U.S.A. by
RR Donnelley Roanoke

Library of Congress Cataloging-in-Publication Data
Gray, Tanis.

 3 skeins or less : fresh knitted accessories / Tanis Gray.

pages cm.

Includes index.

ISBN 978-1-62033-673-1 (pbk.)

ISBN 978-1-62033-674-8 (PDF)

1. Knitting--Patterns. I. Title.
II. Title: Three skeins or less, fresh knitted accessories.

TT825.G658 2014

746.43'2--dc23

2014013491

10 9 8 7 6 5 4 3 2 1

For Mom and Dad, who helped lay a strong foundation and construct the framework of my life, and who provided me with the materials I needed to build my dream.

I am honored to be in the company of such talented and clever knitters, without whom this book would simply not have been possible. You rose to the challenge and together we inspired each other.

To Erica Smith, my fearless editor and amazing friend, my deepest gratitude. You took my blueprints and notes, polished them, and helped me build something grand.

To Kristen TenDyke, a heartfelt thanks for your tech-editing genius.

Thank you to editorial director Allison Korleski for taking my idea and making it a reality.

Many thanks to associate art directors Julia Boyles and Charlene Tiedemann, designer Brenda Gallagher, production designer Kerry Jackson, and photographer Joe Hancock and his team for their talent.

Contents

Introduction

As knitters, we can do a lot with one, two, or even three balls of yarn. A pair of socks or stunning lace shawl out of a singular, stunning hank of yarn? No problem! A sweater out of three skeins? Bring it on! Crafters are curious by nature, and I often challenge myself to knit something with limited yardage.

The process of knitting is magical. We take needles and yarn and create something functional and beautiful. We get to wear what we create with the added bonus of it keeping us warm, making us feel creative, and giving us the satisfaction of stating, when complimented on our hand-knits, "Thanks. I made it and only used one ball of yarn!"

I have found in talking to other knitters that we all love small manageable projects. We live in a fast-paced world, commuting on trains and buses, flying across the world, watching our children at team practice, going to the movies, waiting in the doctor's office, and every now and then getting a quiet moment to sit with our knitting and become one with the fiber and smooth needles clicking away. Small projects are ideal for our hectic lives, but small certainly does not equal boring.

I challenged a group of designers to come up with something grand using just one, two, or three hanks of yarn, and they happily stepped up to the plate. Need a lace fix? Knit up Romi Hill's gorgeous beaded lace shawl or Judy Marples's asymmetrical triangle. Going on vacation somewhere warm? Knit up Sauniell Connally's elegant lace cami or bring it with you on the plane. Need some new socks? Try Glenna Harris's twisted cabled pair or satiate your Latvian Braid craving with Ann Weaver's wristers. Everything in this collection is designed to be portable, so you can knit wherever you may be, and you won't break the bank.

I hope you enjoy the following designs by modern busy knitters. Knitting with only one, two, or three hanks of yarn? Mission accomplished!

Tanis Gray

Interessere STOLE

Entrelac and lace come together in this intricate stole. Three different lace patterns are woven together throughout the body, while a graceful lace edging adorns the top and bottom.

Finished Size
About 55" (139.5 cm) long and 16" (40.5 cm) wide.

Yarn
Lace weight (#1 Super Fine)
Shown here: Tanis Fiber Arts Pink Label Lace Weight (100% superwash merino; 1000 yd [914 m]/115 g): jewel, 1 hank.

Needles
U.S. size 3 (3.25 mm): 24" (60 cm) circular (cir).

Adjust needle size if necessary to obtain the correct gauge.

Notions
Waste yarn; U.S. size G (4 mm) crochet hook; markers (m); tapestry needle.

Gauge
17 sts = 2½" (6.5 cm) and 34 rows = 3¼" (8.5 cm) in Grace, Flower, and Leaf charts.

HEATHER ZOPPETTI

NOTES

✪ Stole is worked using the entrelac technique. The short ends are trimmed with knitted-on borders. A circular needle is used for ease of working.

✪ This pattern uses three lace charts, one per tier. The sample uses the charts in the following order: grace, leaf, flower (see diagram on page 11). The instructions give the basic pattern without specifying which chart to work on a given tier. For base and side triangles, the chart should be worked as best possible, making sure to match each yarnover to its corresponding decrease. If this is not possible, work the extra stitch(es) in stockinette.

Stole

Using the crochet-chain provisional method (see Techniques), CO 78 sts. Do not join.

Set-up row: (WS) K5, place marker (pm), purl to last 5 sts, pm, k5.

BASE TRIANGLES

First triangle:

Row 1: (RS) K5, sl m, work 1 st foll chart (see diagram and Notes), turn.

Row 2: Work 1 st, turn.

Rows 3-4: Work 2 sts, turn.

Rows 5-6: Work 3 sts, turn.

Rows 7-8: Work 4 sts, turn.

Rows 9-10: Work 5 sts, turn.

Rows 11-12: Work 6 sts, turn.

Rows 13-14: Work 7 sts, turn.

Rows 15-16: Work 8 sts, turn.

Rows 17-18: Work 9 sts, turn.

Rows 19-20: Work 10 sts, turn.

Rows 21-22: Work 11 sts, turn.

Rows 23-24: Work 12 sts, turn.

Rows 25-26: Work 13 sts, turn.

Rows 27-28: Work 14 sts, turn.

Rows 29-30: Work 15 sts, turn.

Rows 31-32: Work 16 sts, turn.

Row 33: Work 17 sts, do not turn.

Next 2 triangles:

Row 1: (RS) Work 1 st foll chart, turn.

Work Rows 2-33 as for first triangle.

Rep Rows 1-33 once more—3 triangles complete.

Last triangle:

Work Rows 1-32 as for second and third triangles.

Row 33: Work 17 sts, sl m, k5. Turn.

Key

- ☐ k on RS; p on WS
- ○ yo
- ╱ k2tog
- ╲ ssk
- ⼊ k3tog
- ⋀ sl 2 as if to k2tog, k1, p2sso

Grace

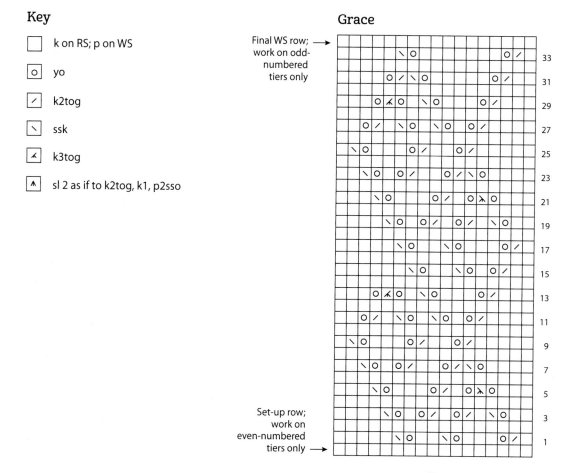

Final WS row; work on odd-numbered tiers only →

Set-up row; work on even-numbered tiers only →

17 sts

Flower

Final WS row;
work on odd-
numbered
tiers only

Set-up row (WS);
work on even-
numbered
tiers only

33
31
29
27
25
23
21
19
17
15
13
11
9
7
5
3
1

17 sts

Leaf

Final WS row;
work on odd-
numbered
tiers only

Set-up row;
work on
even-numbered
tiers only

33
31
29
27
25
23
21
19
17
15
13
11
9
7
5
3
1

17 sts

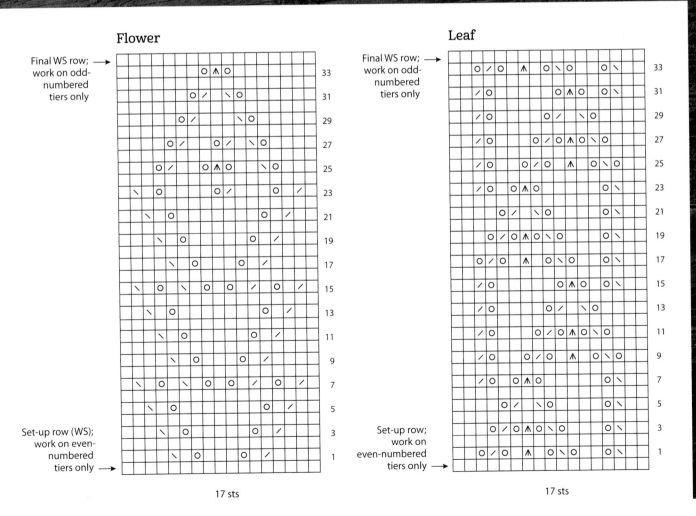

TIER 1: LEFT TO RIGHT

Left side triangle:

Row 1: (WS) K5, sl m, p1, turn.

Row 2: K1f&b (see Techniques) (counts as Row 1 of lace chart), sl m, k5.

Row 3: K5, sl m, work 1 st foll chart, p2tog, turn.

Row 4: K1f&b, work 1 st, sl m, k5.

Row 5: K5, sl m, work to 1 st before previous turn, p2tog, turn.

Row 6: Work to 2 sts before m, k1f&b, work 1 st, sl m, k5.

Rep Rows 5–6 thirteen more times.

Next row: (WS) K5, sl m, work to 1 st before previous turn, p2tog, do not turn.

Right-leaning rectangle:

With WS facing, pick up and purl 17 sts along selvedge edge between needles.

Row 1: (RS) Work 17 sts foll chart, turn.

Row 2: Work 16 sts, p2tog, turn.

Rep Rows 1–2 sixteen more times; do not turn at end of last row.

Work 2 more right-leaning rectangles —3 rectangles total.

Right side triangle:

With WS facing, pick up and purl 17 sts along selvedge edge between needles, sl m, k5.

Row 1: (RS) K5, sl m, work 17 sts foll chart, turn.

Row 2: Work to 2 sts before m, p2tog, sl m, k5.

Row 3: K5, sl m, knit to previous turn, turn.

Rep Rows 2–3 fourteen more times.

Next row: (WS) P2tog, sl m, k5.

Next row: (RS) K5, sl m, k1, do not turn.

TIER 2: RIGHT TO LEFT

Left-leaning rectangle:

With RS facing, pick up and knit 16 sts along selvedge edge between needles, turn—17 sts.

Row 1: (WS) Work 17 sts foll chart, turn.

Row 2: Work 16 sts, ssk, turn.

Rep Rows 1–2 sixteen more times; do not turn at end of last row.

Work 3 more left-leaning rectangles, picking up and knitting 17 sts rather than 16—4 rectangles total. With RS facing, sl m, k5.

TIERS 3–23

[Work tier 1, then tier 2] 10 times, then work tier 1 once more.

Ending Triangles:

With RS facing, pick up and knit 16 sts along selvedge edge between needles, turn—17 sts.

Key

☐	k on RS; p on WS
·	p on RS; k on WS
o	yo
╱	k2tog on RS; p2tog on WS
╲	ssk on RS; ssp on WS
↗	k2tog on WS
↖	ssk on WS (last st of edging tog with 1 shawl st)
⅄	k3tog
⅄	sl 1, k2tog, psso

Border

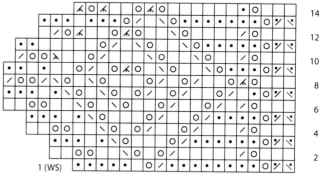

19 sts

Row 1: (WS) Work 17 sts foll chart, turn.

Row 2: Work 16 sts, ssk, turn.

Row 3: Work to 1 st before previous turn, turn.

Row 4: Work to 1 st before previous turn, ssk, turn.

Rep Rows 3–4 fifteen more times; do not turn at end of last row.

Work 3 more ending triangles, picking up and knitting 17 sts rather than 16—4 triangles total. With RS facing, sl m, k5.

TOP BORDER

With RS facing, using the backward-loop method (see Techniques), CO 19 sts—97 sts. Turn.

Row 1: (WS) K18, ssk (1 st from border tog with 1 shawl st), turn—1 st dec'd.

Row 2: K19.

Rep Rows 1–2 two more times, then Row 1 once—93 sts rem.

Work Rows 1–14 of Border chart 10 times—23 sts rem.

Next row: (WS) K18, ssk, turn—1 st dec'd.

Next row: K19.

Rep the last 2 rows two more times, then WS row once—19 sts rem.

BO all sts loosely.

BOTTOM BORDER

Remove waste yarn from provisional cast-on and place these 78 sts on needle. With RS facing, join yarn at left edge of work, then use the backward-loop method to CO 19 sts—97 sts. Turn. Complete as for top border.

Finishing

Block. Weave in ends.

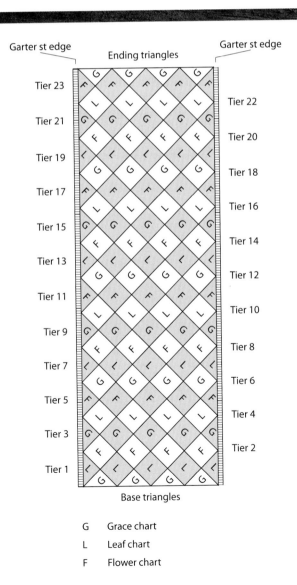

Ending triangles

Garter st edge

Garter st edge

Tier 23
Tier 22
Tier 21
Tier 20
Tier 19
Tier 18
Tier 17
Tier 16
Tier 15
Tier 14
Tier 13
Tier 12
Tier 11
Tier 10
Tier 9
Tier 8
Tier 7
Tier 6
Tier 5
Tier 4
Tier 3
Tier 2
Tier 1

Base triangles

G   Grace chart

L   Leaf chart

F   Flower chart

Annular MITTS

Most patterns that incorporate Latvian braids only include one or two around the cuff of a mitten and leave you wanting more. These mitts are all about braids, which create a dense intricate fabric.

ANN WEAVER

Finished Size

About 6¾ (7¾)" (17 [19.5] cm) hand circumference.

Mitts shown measure 6¾" (17 cm).

Yarn

Fingering weight (#1 Super Fine)

Shown here: Spud & Chloë Fine (80% superwash wool, 20% silk; 248 yd [227 m]/50 g): #7806 calypso (aqua) (MC), 1 hank; #7802 clementine (orange) (CC), 1 hank.

Needles

U.S. size 1 (2.25 mm): set of 4 double-pointed (dpn).

Adjust needle size if necessary to obtain the correct gauge.

Notions

Markers (m); waste yarn; tapestry needle.

Gauge

36 sts and 48 rows = 4" (10 cm) in St st.

NOTES

✪ Mitts are worked in the round from the cuff up.

✪ Do not cut yarns at color changes. Carry unused color loosely up wrong side of work until it is needed again.

✪ Your yarns will twist around each other as you work Round 2 of the braids, then untwist themselves on Round 3.

Right-Leaning Single-Stitch Braid: (even number of sts)

Rnd 1: *K1 with MC, k1 with CC; rep from * to end.

Rnd 2: Bring both yarns to front of work. *With MC, p1 bringing strand under CC strand; with CC, p1 bringing strand under MC strand; rep from * to end.

Rnd 3: Leave both yarns in front. *With MC, p1 bringing strand over CC strand; with CC, p1 bringing strand over MC strand; rep from * to end.

Left-Leaning Single-Stitch Braid: (even number of sts)

Rnd 1: *K1 with MC, k1 with CC; rep from * to end.

Rnd 2: Bring both yarns to front of work. *With MC, p1 bringing yarn over CC strand; with CC, p1 bringing yarn over MC strand; rep from * to end.

Rnd 3: Leave both yarns in front. *With MC, p1 bringing strand under CC strand; with CC, p1 bringing yarn under MC strand; rep from * to end.

Right-Leaning Double-Stitch Braid: (multiple of 4 sts)

Rnd 1: *K2 with MC, k2 with CC; rep from * to end.

Rnd 2: Bring both yarns to front of work. *With MC, p2 bringing strand under CC strand; with CC, p2 bringing strand under MC strand; rep from * to end.

Rnd 3: Leave both yarns in front. *With MC, p2 bringing strand over CC strand; with CC, p2 bringing strand over MC strand; rep from * to end.

Left-Leaning Double-Stitch Braid: (multiple of 4 sts)

Rnd 1: *K2 with MC, k2 with CC; rep from * to end.

Rnd 2: Bring both yarns to front of work. *With MC, p2 bringing strand over CC strand; with CC, p2 bringing strand over MC strand; rep from * to end.

Rnd 3: Leave both yarns in front. *With MC, p2 bringing strand under CC strand; with CC, p2 bringing strand under MC strand; rep from * to end.

Right Mitt

CUFF

With MC, CO 60 (68) sts. Place marker (pm) and join to work in the round, being careful not to twist sts. Knit 1 rnd.

Join CC. Work Right-Leaning Single-Stitch Braid.

With MC, knit 3 rnds. Work Left-Leaning Single-Stitch Braid. Work Right-Leaning Double-Stitch Braid. Work Left-Leaning Single-Stitch Braid.

With CC, knit 3 rnds. Work Right-Leaning Double-Stitch Braid.

With CC, knit 3 rnds. Work Left-Leaning Single-Stitch Braid. Work Right-Leaning Double-Stitch Braid. Work Left-Leaning Single-Stitch Braid.

THUMB GUSSET

Rnd 1: With MC, k44 (48), pm for gusset, M1R (see Techniques), k1, M1L (see Techniques), pm for gusset, knit to end—62 (70) sts; 3 sts between gusset m.

Rnd 2: With MC, knit.

Rnd 3: With MC, knit to first m, sl m, M1R, knit to second m, M1L, sl m, knit to end—2 sts inc'd.

Rep Rnds 2-3 once more—66 (74) sts; 7 sts between gusset m.

Work Right-Leaning Single-Stitch Braid.

Inc rnd: With CC, knit to first m, sl m, M1R, knit to second m, M1L, sl m, knit to end—2 sts inc'd.

Next rnd: With CC, knit.

Rep the last 2 rnds once more, then Inc rnd once—72 (80) sts; 13 sts between gusset m.

Work Left-Leaning Single-Stitch Braid.

Inc rnd: With MC, knit to first m, sl m, M1R, knit to second m, M1L, sl m, knit to end—2 sts inc'd.

Next rnd: With MC, knit.

Rep the last 2 rnds once more, then Inc rnd once—78 (86) sts; 19 sts between gusset m.

Work Right-Leaning Single-Stitch Braid.

Inc rnd: With CC, knit to first m, sl m, M1R, knit to second m, M1L, sl m, knit to end—2 sts inc'd.

Next rnd: With CC, knit.

Rep the last 2 rnds once more, then Inc rnd once—84 (92) sts; 25 sts between gusset m.

Work Left-Leaning Single-Stitch Braid.

With MC, knit 5 rnds.

Work Right-Leaning Single-Stitch Braid.

Next rnd: With CC, knit to first m, remove m, place next 25 sts on waste yarn for thumb, remove m, CO 5 sts, knit to end—64 (72) sts.

HAND

With CC, knit 4 rnds. Work Left-Leaning Single-Stitch Braid.

With MC, knit 5 rnds. Work Right-Leaning Single-Stitch Braid. Work Left-Leaning Double-Stitch Braid. Work Right-Leaning Single-Stitch Braid.

With CC, knit 3 rnds. Work Left-Leaning Single-Stitch Braid.

With CC, knit 3 rnds. Work Right-Leaning Single-Stitch Braid.

With MC, knit 1 rnd.

With MC and using the sewn bind-off (see Techniques), BO all sts.

THUMB

Place 25 held sts on dpn. Join CC, k25, pick up and knit 3 sts from CO edge, pm for beg of rnd, pick up and knit 2 sts from CO edge—30 sts.

With CC, knit 4 rnds. Join MC.

Work Left-Leaning Single Stitch Braid.

With MC, knit 1 rnd.

With MC and using the sewn bind-off, BO all sts.

Left Mitt

CUFF

With MC, CO 60 (68) sts. Place marker (pm) and join to work in the round, being careful not to twist sts. Knit 1 rnd.

Join CC. Work Left-Leaning Single-Stitch Braid.

With MC, knit 3 rnds. Work Right-Leaning Single-Stitch Braid. Work Left-Leaning Double-Stitch Braid. Work Right-Leaning Single-Stitch Braid.

With CC, knit 3 rnds. Work Left-Leaning Single-Stitch Braid.

With CC, knit 3 rnds. Work Right-Leaning Single-Stitch Braid. Work Left-Leaning Double-Stitch Braid. Work Right-Leaning Single-Stitch Braid.

THUMB GUSSET

Rnd 1: With MC, k15 (19), pm for gusset, M1R, k1, M1L, pm for gusset, knit to end—62 (70) sts; 3 sts between gusset m.

Rnd 2: With MC, knit.

Rnd 3: With MC, knit to first m, sl m, M1R, knit to m, M1L, sl m, knit to end—2 sts inc'd.

Rep Rnds 2–3 once more—66 (74) sts; 7 sts between gusset m.

Work Left-Leaning Single-Stitch Braid.

Inc rnd: With CC, knit to first m, sl m, M1R, knit to second m, M1L, sl m, knit to end—2 sts inc'd.

Next rnd: With CC, knit.

Rep the last 2 rnds once more, then Inc rnd once—72 (80) sts; 13 sts between gusset m.

Work Right-Leaning Single-Stitch Braid.

Inc rnd: With MC, knit to first m, sl m, M1R, knit to second m, M1L, sl m, knit to end—2 sts inc'd.

Next rnd: With MC, knit.

Rep the last 2 rnds once more, then Inc rnd once—78 (86) sts; 19 sts between gusset m.

Work Left-Leaning Single-Stitch Braid.

Inc rnd: With CC, knit to first m, sl m, M1R, knit to second m, M1L, sl m, knit to end—2 sts inc'd.

Next rnd: With CC, knit.

Rep the last 2 rnds once more, then Inc rnd once—84 (92) sts; 25 sts between gusset m.

Work Right-Leaning Single-Stitch Braid.

With MC, knit 5 rnds.

Work Left-Leaning Single-Stitch Braid.

Next rnd: With CC, knit to first m, remove m, place next 25 sts on waste yarn for thumb, remove m, CO 5 sts, knit to end—64 (72) sts.

HAND

With CC, knit 4 rnds. Work Right-Leaning Single-Stitch Braid.

With MC, knit 5 rnds. Work Left-Leaning Single-Stitch Braid. Work Right-Leaning Double-Stitch Braid. Work Left-Leaning Single-Stitch Braid.

With CC, knit 3 rnds. Work Right-Leaning Single-Stitch Braid.

With CC, knit 3 rnds. Work Left-Leaning Single-Stitch Braid.

With MC, knit 1 rnd.

With MC and using the sewn bind-off, BO all sts.

THUMB

Place 25 held sts on dpn. Join CC, k25, pick up and knit 3 sts from CO edge, pm for beg of rnd, pick up and knit 2 sts from CO edge—30 sts.

With CC, knit 4 rnds. Join MC.

Work Right-Leaning Single Stitch Braid.

With MC, knit 1 rnd.

With MC and using the sewn bind-off, BO all sts.

Finishing

Weave in ends. Block.

Diverting SOCKS

These socks are for those days when you want to feel the sturdy comfort of cables as you rush about your busy day. Even if the cables are mostly hidden, you'll know they're there. They're also fun to knit, keeping your attention focused when you need a few moments of diversion.

Finished Size
About 7 (8)" (18 [20.5] cm) foot circumference.

Socks shown measure 7" (18 cm).

Yarn
Fingering weight (#1 Super Fine)

Shown here: Dream in Color Everlasting Sock (100% superwash merino wool; 420 yd [384 m]/100 g): chili, 1 hank

Needles
U.S. size 1½ (2.5 mm): set of 4 double-pointed (dpn).

Adjust needle size if necessary to achieve the correct gauge.

Notions
Markers (m); cable needle (cn); tapestry needle.

Gauge
32 sts and 44 rows = 4" (10 cm) in St st.

GLENNA HARRIS

NOTE

✪ These socks are worked from the cuff down with a flap heel. Socks are made mirror images of each other by beginning at different points in the cable pattern.

First Sock

CUFF

CO 68 (76) sts, place marker (pm) and join to work in the round, taking care not to twist sts.

Size 7" (18 cm) only:

Rnd 1: *P1, k4, [p2, k2] 2 times, p4, k4, p4, k2, p2, k4, p1; rep from * once more.

Size 8" (20.5 cm) only:

Rnd 1: *K2, p1, k4, [p2, k2] 2 times, p4, k4, p4, k2, p2, k4, p1, k2; rep from * once more.

Both sizes:

Rep last rnd 11 more times.

LEG

Size 7" (18 cm) only:

Rnd 1: Work Rnd 1 of Cable chart.

Size 8" (20.5 cm) only:

Rnd 1: *K2, work Rnd 1 of Cable chart over 34 sts, k2; rep from * once more.

Both sizes:

Cont in patt, work Rnds 2–24 of Cable chart, then Rnds 1–24 once, then Rnds 1–15 once. Sock measures about 7" (18 cm) from CO.

HEEL FLAP

Heel flap is worked over first 34 (38) sts. Set rem 34 (38) instep sts aside.

Size 7" (18 cm) only:

Row 1: (RS) Sl 1 pwise, k4, p2, k2, p4, k2, p2, k4, p4, k2, p2, k4, p1, turn.

Row 2: (WS) Sl 1 pwise, p4, k2, p2, k4, p4, k2, p2, k4, p2, k2, p4, k1, turn.

Size 8" (20.5 cm) only:

Row 1: (RS) Sl 1 pwise, k5, p2, k2, p4, k2, p2, k4, p4, k2, p2, k4, p1, k2, turn.

Row 2: (WS) Sl 1 pwise, p1, k1, p4, k2, p2, k4, p4, k2, p2, k4, p2, k2, p6, turn.

Both sizes:

Rep the last 2 rows 15 (17) more times.

Turn heel:

Row 1: (RS) K20 (22), ssk, k1, turn—1 st dec'd.

Row 2: Sl 1 pwise, p7, p2tog, p1, turn—1 st dec'd.

Row 3: Sl 1 pwise, knit to 1 st before previous turn, ssk, k1, turn—1 st dec'd.

Row 4: Sl 1 pwise, purl to 1 st before previous turn, p2tog, p1, turn—1 st dec'd.

Rep the last 2 rows four (five) more times—22 (24) sts rem.

Next row: (RS) Sl 1 pwise, knit to last 2 sts, ssk, turn—21 (23) sts rem.

Next row: Sl 1 pwise, purl to last 2 sts, p2tog, turn—20 (22) sts rem.

GUSSET

Rnd 1: K20 (22) heel sts, pick up and knit 17 (19) sts from left side of heel flap, pm, work in established cable patt across 34 (38) instep sts, pm, pick up and knit 17 (19) sts from right side of heel flap, k10 (11) to middle of heel, pm for new beg of rnd—88 (98) sts.

Rnd 2: Knit to m, sl m, work in patt across instep to m, sl m, knit to end.

Rnd 3: Knit to 3 sts before instep m, k2tog, k1, sl m, work in patt to m, sl m, k1, ssk, knit to end—2 sts dec'd.

Rep the last 2 rnds nine (ten) more times—68 (76) sts rem; 34 (38) sts for sole and 34 (38) for instep.

FOOT

Work even until foot from back of heel measures about 2 (2¼)" (5 [5.5] cm) less than desired total length.

TOE

Rnd 1: Knit to 3 sts before instep m, k2tog, k1, sl m, k1, ssk, work sts as they appear (knit the knit sts and purl the purl sts) to 3 sts before next m, k2tog, k1, sm, k1, ssk, knit to end—4 sts dec'd.

Rnd 2: Work even.

Rep the last 2 rnds ten (twelve) more times—24 sts rem.

Divide sts so 12 sole sts are on one needle and 12 instep sts are on a second needle. Graft toe closed using Kitchener st (see Techniques).

Second Sock

CUFF

CO 68 (76) sts, place marker (pm) and join to work in the round, taking care not to twist sts.

Size 7" (18 cm) only:

Rnd 1: *P1, k4, p2, k2, p4, k4, p4, [k2, p2] twice, k4, p1; rep from * once more.

Size 8" (20.5 cm) only:

Rnd 1: *K2, p1, k4, p2, k2, p4, k4, p4, [k2, p2] twice, k4, p1, k2; rep from * once more.

Both sizes:

Rep last rnd 11 more times.

Key

☐	k on RS; p on WS
⊡	p on RS; k on WS
⧄⧄	sl 2 sts onto cn, hold in back, k2, k2 from cn
⧅⧅	sl 2 sts onto cn, hold in front, k2, k2 from cn
◢	sl 2 sts onto cn, hold in back, k2, p2 from cn
◣	sl 2 sts onto cn, hold in front, p2, k2 from cn
☐	pattern repeat

Cable

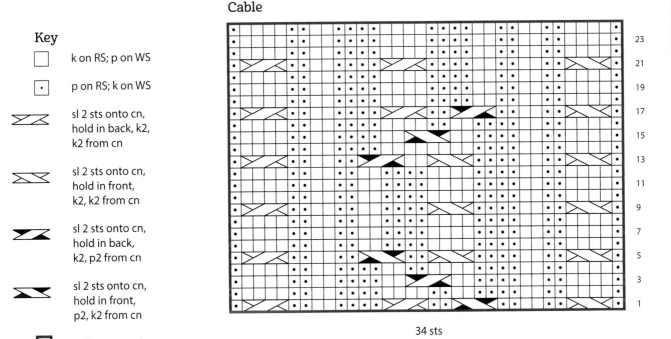

34 sts

23
21
19
17
15
13
11
9
7
5
3
1

LEG

Size 7" (18 cm) only:

Rnd 1: Work Rnd 13 of Cable chart.

Size 8" (20.5 cm) only:

Rnd 1: *K2, work Rnd 13 of Cable chart over 34 sts, k2; rep from * once more.

Both sizes:

Cont in patt, work Rnds 14–24 of Cable chart, then Rnds 1–24 once, then Rnds 1–3. Sock measures about 7" (18 cm) from CO.

HEEL FLAP

Heel flap is worked over first 34 (38) sts. Set rem 34 (38) instep sts aside.

Size 7" (18 cm) only:

Row 1: (RS) Sl 1 pwise, k4, p2, k2, p4, k4, p2, k2, p4, k2, p2, k4, p1, turn.

Row 2: (WS) Sl 1 pwise, p4, k2, p2, k4, p2, k2, p4, k4, p2, k2, p4, k1, turn.

Size 8" (20.5 cm) only:

Row 1: (RS) Sl 1 pwise, k1, p1, k4, p2, k2, p4, k4, p2, k2, p4, k2, p2, k4, p1, k2, turn.

Row 2: (WS) Sl 1 pwise, p1, k1, p4, k2, p2, k4, p2, k2, p4, k4, p2, k2, p4, k1, p2, turn.

Complete as for first sock.

Finishing

Weave in ends. Block if desired.

Colorblock HAT

3 SKEINS

Knitting a colorblock hat with a rustic tweed yarn on an early fall day is one of the best things to do that time of year. The basic shape of the hat makes the perfect setting for simple two-color stranded color blocks, and the stranded sections carry the bonus of making the hat doubly warm. The Colorblock Hat whips up in no time and the sections of colorwork squares keep your interest at a peak.

Finished Size
18¼" (46.5 cm) circumference.

Yarn
Worsted weight (#4 Medium)

Shown here: BrooklynTweed Shelter (100% Targhee–Columbia wool; 140 yd [128 m]/50 g): #28 sweatshirt (gray) (MC), 1 hank; #20 cast iron (black) (CC1), 1 hank; #23 fossil (off-white) (CC2), 1 hank.

Needles
U.S. size 7 (4.5 mm): 16" (40 cm) circular (cir) and set of 4 double-pointed (dpn).

Adjust needle size if necessary to obtain the correct gauge.

Notions
Markers (m); tapestry needle.

Gauge
22 sts and 30 rows = 4" (10 cm) in St st; 22 sts and 28 rows = 4" (10 cm) in stranded color work.

SUSAN B. ANDERSON

NOTE

✪ Hat is worked in the round in stranded color work. Carry color not in use loosely across the wrong side of the work. When it is necessary to carry the yarn for more than 1" (2.5 cm), as in Rnds 1–10 of pattern, it's best to tack down the long floats (see page 27).

Hat

BRIM

With MC and cir needle, CO 100 sts. Place marker (pm) and join for working in the round, being careful not to twist sts. Work in k1, p1 rib for 1½" (4 cm). Cut MC. Join CC1 and CC2.

BODY

Rnds 1–10: *K10 with CC1, k10 with CC2 (see Notes); rep from * to end.

Cut CC1 and CC2. Join MC.

Rnds 11–13: With MC, knit.

Cut MC. Join CC1 and CC2.

Rnds 14–18: *K5 with CC2, k5 with CC1; rep from * to end.

Rnds 19–23: *K5 with CC1, k5 with CC2; rep from * to end.

Cut CC1 and CC2. Join MC.

Rnds 24–26: With MC, knit.

Cut MC. Join CC1 and CC2.

Rnds 27–28: *K2 with CC2, k2 with CC1; rep from * to end.

Rnds 29–30: *K2 with CC1, k2 with CC2; rep from * to end.

Rnds 31–32: Rep Rnds 27–28.

Rnds 33–34: Rep Rnds 29–30.

Rnds 35–36: Rep Rnds 27–28.

Cut CC1 and CC2. Join MC.

Knit 2 rnds. Hat measures about 7" (18 cm) from CO.

CROWN

Note: Change to dpns when there are too few sts to work comfortably on cir needle.

Set-up rnd: *K1, k2tog, k19, ssk, k1, pm; rep from * to end—92 sts rem.

Knit 1 rnd.

Dec rnd: *K1, k2tog, knit to 3 sts before m, ssk, k1, sl m; rep from * to end—8 sts dec'd.

Rep last 2 rnds 8 more times—20 sts rem.

Next rnd: *K2tog, k1, ssk; rep from * to end—12 sts rem.

Break yarn, leaving a 6" (15 cm) tail. Thread tail onto tapestry needle and draw through rem sts, pull snug to tighten, and fasten off inside.

Finishing

Weave in ends. Block.

TWISTS (MAKE 2)

Cut 60" (152.5 cm) lengths of MC, CC1, and CC2. Holding 3 strands together, make a twisted cord (see opposite page). Sew to the top of the hat.

MAKING A
TWISTED CORD

Cut several lengths of yarn about five times the desired finished cord length. Fold the strands in half to form two equal groups. Anchor the strands at the fold by looping them over a doorknob. Holding one group in each hand, twist each group tightly in a clockwise direction until they begin to kink. Put both groups in one hand, then release them, allowing them to twist around each other counterclockwise. Smooth out the twists so that they are uniform along the length of the cord. Knot the ends.

TACKING DOWN
LONG FLOATS

To prevent long floats that can catch on fingers and distort the stitches, floats should be no longer than 1" (2.5 cm) long. If a float needs to span a wider distance, it's best to trap or "catch" it with the working yarn to keep it snug against the back of the work.

To trap a long float against the back of the fabric, insert the needle tip into the next stitch on the left-hand needle, place the nonworking yarnover the right needle (**Figure 1;** nonworking yarn is dark), knit the stitch with the working yarn as usual, then lower the nonworking yarn (**Figure 2**) and knit the following stitch as usual.

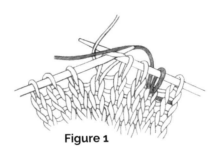

Figure 1

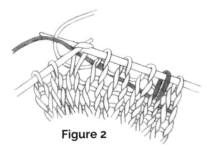

Figure 2

Eline COWL

This cowl is fun, fast, and versatile enough to make in different yarns, different fibers, different colors—the only thing that limits you is your imagination. Two versions are included here to pique your curiosity!

VERSION 1

Finished Size

About 24" (61 cm) in circumference and 40" (101.5 cm) tall.

Yarn

Fingering weight (#1 Super Fine)

Shown here: Classic Elite Yarns Alpaca Sox (60% alpaca, 20% merino wool, 20% nylon; 450 yd [411 m]/100 g): #kettle 1814 dried lavender, 2 hanks.

Needles

U.S. size 6 (4 mm): 40" (100 cm) circular (cir).

Adjust needle size if necessary to obtain the correct gauge.

Notions

Marker (m); waste yarn; tapestry needle.

Gauge

32 sts and 24 rnds = 4" (10 cm) in mesh st.

Gauge is approximate. Mesh patt stretches a great deal both vertically and horizontally.

ÅSA TRICOSA

NOTES

✪ Cowl is worked in the round beginning with a Moebius cast-on (see Techniques) and finished with a picot bind-off.

✪ The fabric will twist in on itself as you knit. Toward the end you'll need to regularly pull the fabric out of the center, bit by bit, to give yourself enough slack to work.

Stitch Guide

S2kp2

Sl 2 sts as if to k2tog, k1, pass 2 sl sts over knit st—2 sts dec'd.

Mesh Stitch

(multiple of 4 sts)

Rnd 1: *Yo, s2kp2, yo, k1; rep from * to end.

Rnd 2: Knit.

Rnd 3: Sl 1, *yo, k1, yo, s2kp2; rep from * to last 3 sts, yo, k1, yo, sl 2 sts as if to k2tog, remove m, k1, pass 2 sl sts over knit st, pm.

Rnd 4: Knit.

Rep Rnds 1–4 for patt.

Cowl (Version 1)

Using the Moebius method (see Techniques), CO 160 sts (counting loops on needle only, not loops on cable).

Work Rnds 1–4 of mesh st 29 times.

EDGING

Rnd 1: *P1, k1; rep from * to end.

Rep last rnd 5 more times.

BO all sts using the picot bind-off as foll: P1, *use the cable method (see Techniques) to CO 1 st, BO 3 sts in patt; rep from * until all sts are bound off.

Finishing

Weave in ends. Soak and block. Because of the Moebius loop, cowl must be blocked with a twist.

Version 2

Finished Size

About 65" (165 cm) in circumference and 28" (71 cm) tall.

Yarn

Lace weight (#0 Lace)

Shown here: Classic Elite Yarns Silky Alpaca Lace (70% alpaca, 30% silk; 440 yd [402 m]/50 g): #2443 apricot, 2 balls.

Needles

U.S. size 4 (3.5 mm): 40" (100 cm) circular (cir).

Adjust needle size if necessary to obtain the correct gauge.

Notions

Marker (m); waste yarn; tapestry needle.

Gauge

40 sts and 20 rnds = 4" (10 cm) in mesh st.

Gauge is approximate. Mesh patt stretches a great deal both vertically and horizontally.

NOTES

✪ Cowl is worked in the round beginning with a Moebius cast on and finished with a simple knitted-on edging.

✪ The fabric will twist in on itself as you knit. Toward the end you'll need to regularly pull the fabric out of the center, bit by bit, to give yourself enough slack to work.

Cowl (Version 2)

Using the Moebius method (see Techniques), CO 320 sts (counting loops on needle only, not loops on cable).

Work Rnds 1–4 of mesh st 14 times.

EDGING

Set-up row: K1, sl 1 st from right needle to left. Using the invisible provisional method (see Techniques), CO 6 sts on left needle.

Row 1: (RS) K5, ssk (last st of edging tog with 1 st of cowl), turn—1 st dec'd.

Row 2: (WS) Sl 1 with yarn in front (wyf), k5.

Row 3: BO 2 sts, k2, ssk (last st of edging tog with 1 st of cowl), turn—1 st dec'd.

Row 4: Sl 1 wyf, k1, [yo] 2 times, k2.

Row 5: K2, [p1, k1] into double yo, k1, ssk (last st of edging tog with 1 st of cowl), turn—1 st dec'd.

Rep Rows 2–5 318 more times, then Row 2 once—6 edging sts and 1 cowl st rem.

Next row (RS): K5, ssk—6 edging sts and no cowl sts rem.

Finishing

Remove waste yarn from provisional CO and place 6 sts on empty needle tip. Use Kitchener st (see Techniques) to graft 6 live edging sts to provisional CO sts.

Weave in ends. Soak and block. Because of the Moebius loop, cowl must be blocked with a twist.

Checkered Past SHRUG

This classic shrug is worked in two pieces from the center back to the wrist with a simple lace and cable repeat that resembles a checkerboard when complete. Garter stitch edges the upper and lower bands and cuffs.

Finished Size
64 (66½, 69)" (162.5 [169, 175.5] cm) from cuff to cuff and 14 (16, 17¾)" (35.5 [40.5, 45] cm) tall at center back.

Shrug shown measures 64" (162.5 cm).

Yarn
Sport weight (#2 Fine)

Shown here: Blue Moon Fiber Arts BFL Sport (100% Blue-Faced Leicester; 661 yd [604 ml]/226 g): Smoke on the Water, 2 (2, 3) hanks.

Needles
U.S. size 5 (3.75 mm): straight.

Adjust needle size if necessary to get the correct gauge.

Notions
Markers (m); cable needle (cn); U.S. size G (4 mm) crochet hook; tapestry needle; waste yarn.

Gauge
26 sts and 40 rows = 4" (10 cm) in Lace and Cable charts.

JOAN FORGIONE

NOTES

✪ Shrug is worked flat beginning with a provisional cast-on (see Techniques) at center back. Each half of the shrug is worked outward from the center back to the cuff.

✪ During shaping, if there are not enough stitches to work each decrease with its companion yarnover, work the remaining stitch(es) in stockinette instead. When shaping decreases occur within the cables, decreases should be in made within the 3 sts that are in back (underneath the crossing), regardless if these are the edge sts of the cable. When there are fewer than 6 sts available for a cable, omit cable and work the remaining stitch(es) in stockinette.

Shrug

LEFT HALF

Using the crochet-chain provisional method (see Techniques), CO 96 (108, 120) sts.

Set-up row: (WS) K12, place marker (pm), purl to last 12 sts, pm, p12.

Set-up row: (RS) Knit to m, sl m, work Left Lace and Cable chart to m, sl m, knit to end.

Cont in patt, keeping sts outside markers in garter st, until piece measures 2¾ (3½, 4¼)" (7 [9, 12] cm) from CO, ending with a WS row.

Shape body:

Dec row: (RS) K12, sl m, ssk, work in patt to 2 sts before m, k2tog, sl m, k12—2 sts dec'd.

Cont to dec 1 st inside m at each end (see Notes) every 16 (26, 36) rows 5 (3, 3) more times, then every 14 (16, 0) rows 2 (2, 0) times—80 (96, 112) sts rem.

Work 1 WS row even.

Dec row: (RS) K1, ssk, work in patt to last 3 sts, k2tog, k1—2 sts dec'd.

Rep Dec row on every RS row 11 more times, removing m when necessary—56 (72, 88) sts rem.

Sleeve:

Keeping 1 st at each end in garter st, work even until piece measures 30¼ (31½, 32¾)" (77 [80, 83] cm) from CO, ending with a WS row. Work in garter st for 1¾" (4.5 cm), ending with a WS row. BO all sts.

RIGHT HALF

Remove waste yarn from CO and place 96 (108, 120) live sts on needle. Join yarn with WS facing.

Complete as for left half, working Right Lace and Cable chart instead of Left Lace and Cable chart.

Finishing

Wet block to schematic measurements. Seam sleeves from cuff to about 18" (45.5 cm), or as desired. Weave in ends.

Left Lace and Cable

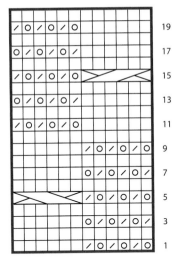

12-st repeat

Right Lace and Cable

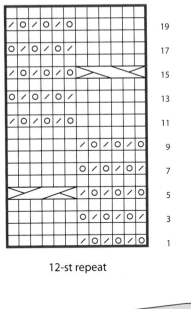

12-st repeat

Key

☐	k on RS; p on WS
⊙	yo
╱	k2tog
☐	pattern repeat
⤬	sl 3 sts onto cn, hold in front, k3, k3 from cn
⤬	sl 3 sts onto cn, hold in back, k3, k3 from cn

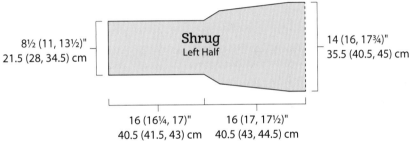

8½ (11, 13½)"
21.5 (28, 34.5) cm

Shrug
Left Half

14 (16, 17¾)"
35.5 (40.5, 45) cm

16 (16¼, 17)"
40.5 (41.5, 43) cm

16 (17, 17½)"
40.5 (43, 44.5) cm

Twigs BOLERO

Envelop yourself in the luxury of this bolero, and revel in the knowledge that you can create a beautiful garment using just a few skeins!

Finished Sizes

34¼ (39, 42¼, 46¾, 51½)" (87 [99, 107.5, 118.5, 131] cm) bust circumference.

Pullover shown measures 34¼" (87 cm).

Yarn

Worsted weight (#4 Medium)

Shown here: Miss Babs Yowza (100% superwash merino; 560 yd [512 m]/225 g): oyster, 2 (2, 2, 3, 3) hanks.

Needles

Body: U.S. size 4 (3.5 mm): 24" (60 cm) circular (cir); U.S. size 5 (3.75 mm): 16" (40 cm) and 24" (60 cm) cirs; U.S. size 6 (4 mm): 24" (60 cm) cir.

Cowl: U.S. size 7 (4.5 mm): 24" (60 cm) cir.

Adjust needle sizes if necessary to obtain the correct gauge.

Notions

Markers (m); tapestry needle; stitch holders.

Gauge

20½ sts and 32 rows = 4" (10 cm) in openwork st on size 6 (4 mm) needle; 22 sts and 36 rows = 4" (10 cm) in openwork st on size 5 (3.75 mm) needle; 23 sts and 40 rows = 4" (10 cm) in openwork st on size 4 (3.75 mm) needle.

FAINA GOBERSTEIN

NOTES

✪ Pullover is worked from the bottom up, in the round to the armholes, then back and front are divided. Additional stitches are cast on for sleeves, then upper back and upper front are worked back-and-forth to the shoulders.

✪ The openwork stitch pattern tends to bias, particularly when worked in the round. Pullover should be blocked carefully to counter this tendency.

✪ When counting stitches in openwork stitch, do not count the yarnovers made on Round/Row 2.

Twisted Backward-Loop Cast-On

*Make a loop by wrapping yarn around left thumb front to back (clockwise); use thumb and index finger to twist this loop counter-clockwise once, then place twisted loop on needle. Rep from *.

Seed Stitch in rnds (odd number of sts)

Rnd 1: K1, *p1, k1; rep from * to end.

Rnd 2: P1, *k1, p1; rep from * to end.

Rep Rnds 1 and 2 for patt.

Openwork Stitch in rnds (multiple of 4 sts)

Rnd 1: Knit.

Rnd 2: *Yo, k4; rep from * to end.

Rnd 3: *Yo, drop yo from previous rnd, sl 1 kwise with yarn in back (wyb), k3, pass sl st over 3 sts; rep from * to end.

Rnd 4: Knit.

Rep Rnds 1–4 for patt.

Openwork Stitch in rows (multiple of 4 sts + 2)

Row 1: (RS) Knit.

Row 2: K1, *p4, yo; rep from * to last st, k1.

Row 3: K1, *yo, drop yo from previous row, sl 1 kwise wyb, k3, pass sl st over 3 sts; rep from * to last st, k1.

Row 4: Purl.

Rep Rows 1–4 for patt.

Bolero

BODY

With size 6 (4 mm) needle, CO 177 (201, 217, 241, 265) sts. Place marker (pm) and join to work in the rnd, taking care not to twist sts.

Change to size 4 (3.5 mm) needle. Work in seed st for 10 rnds, dec 1 st on last rnd—176 (200, 216, 240, 264) sts rem.

Work in openwork st worked in rnds for 4 rnds.

Change to longer size 5 (3.75 mm) needle. Cont in patt until body measures 3" (7.5 cm) from CO.

Change to size 6 (4 mm) needle. Cont in patt until body measures 7 (7, 7, 7½, 7½)" (18 [18, 18, 19, 19] cm) from CO, ending with Rnd 4 of patt.

UPPER BACK

Divide front and back: (RS) Work 88 (100, 108, 120, 132) sts in patt and place on holder for front, work in patt to end. Do not turn. Using the twisted backward-loop method (see Stitch Guide), CO 41 (41, 45, 45, 45) sts for left sleeve—129 (141, 153, 165, 177) sts. Turn to begin working back and forth in rows.

Next row: (WS) K1, *p4, yo; rep from * to end. Do not turn. Using the twisted backward-loop method, CO 41 (41, 45, 45, 45) sts for right sleeve—170 (182, 198, 210, 220) sts.

Beg with Row 3 of patt, cont in openwork st worked in rows until piece measures 6¾ (7½, 8, 8½, 8¾)" (17 [19, 20.5, 21.5, 22] cm) from sleeve CO, ending with Row 2 of patt.

Shape neck:

Next row: (RS) Work 67 (73, 77, 81, 87) sts in patt (see Notes), join a second ball of yarn and BO 36 (36, 44, 48, 48) sts for neck, work in patt to end—67 (73, 77, 81, 87) sts rem for each shoulder.

Working both sides at the same time with separate balls of yarn, work 5 rows even. Place sts on holders.

UPPER FRONT

Place 88 (100, 108, 120, 132) held front sts on size 6 (4 mm) needle and join yarn with WS facing.

Next row: (WS) Use the knitted CO method (see Techniques) to CO 41 (41, 45, 45, 45) sts for right sleeve, k1, *p4, yo; rep from * to end. Do not turn. Use the twisted backward-loop method to CO 41 (41, 45, 45, 45) sts for left sleeve—170 (182, 198, 210, 220) sts.

Beg with Row 3 of patt, cont in openwork st worked in rows until piece measures 4 (4¼, 4¼, 4½, 4½)" (10 [11, 11, 11.5, 11.5] cm) from sleeve CO, ending with a WS row.

Shape neck:

Next row: (RS) Work 79 (85, 91, 97, 103) sts in patt and place on a holder for left side, BO 12 (12, 16, 16, 16) sts for neck, work to end—79 (85, 91, 97, 103) sts rem for right side.

Right side:

Work 1 WS row even.

Next row: (RS) BO 2 (2, 3, 3, 3) sts, work to end—77 (83, 88, 94, 100) sts rem.

Dec row: (WS) Work to last 3 sts, p2tog, k1—1 st dec'd.

Next row: Sl 1, work to end.

Rep the last 2 rows 9 (9, 10, 12, 12) more times—67 (73, 77, 81, 87) sts rem.

Work even until piece measures 7½ (8¼, 8¾, 9¼, 9½)" (19 [21, 22, 23.5, 24] cm) from sleeve CO, ending with Row 4 of patt.

Place sts on a holder.

Left side:

Place 79 (85, 91, 97, 103) held left side sts on size 6 (4 mm) needle and join yarn with WS facing.

Next row: (WS) BO 2 (2, 3, 3, 3) sts, work to end—77 (83, 88, 94, 100) sts rem.

Dec row: (RS) Work to last 3 sts, k2tog, k1—1 st dec'd.

Next row: Sl 1, work to end.

Rep the last 2 rows 9 (9, 10, 12, 12) more times—67 (73, 77, 81, 87) sts rem.

Work even until piece measures 7½ (8¼, 8¾, 9¼, 9½)" (19 [21, 22, 23.5, 24] cm) from sleeve CO, ending with Row 4 of patt.

Place sts on a holder.

Finishing

Weave in ends. Block to schematic measurements. With right sides facing, join shoulders using a 3-needle BO (see Techniques). Sew sleeve underarm seams.

SLEEVE TRIM

With RS facing, beg at underarm seam and using shorter size 5 (3.75 mm) cir needle, pick up and knit 77 (83, 89, 95, 97) sts around sleeve opening. Pm for beg of rnd. Work in seed st for 5 rnds. BO loosely in patt.

COWL

With WS facing, beg at left shoulder seam and using size 6 (4 mm) cir needle, pick up and knit 46 (46, 54, 58, 58) sts across back neck, 26 (30, 33, 35, 37) sts from right front neck, 13 (13, 17, 17, 17) sts across center front neck, and 26 (30, 33, 35, 37) sts from left front neck—111 (119, 137, 145, 149) sts. Pm for beg of rnd.

Change to size 4 (3.5 mm) needle. Work in seed st until cowl measures 1½" (4 cm) from pick-up rnd.

Change to size 5 (3.75 mm) needle. Cont in patt until cowl measures 3" (8 cm) from pick-up rnd.

Change to size 6 (4 mm) needle. Cont in patt until cowl measures 5" (12.5 cm) from pick-up rnd.

Change to size 7 (4.5 mm) needle. Cont in patt until cowl measures 6" (15 cm) from pick-up rnd.

Knit 7 rnds.

BO all sts very loosely.

Weave in ends. Gently steam-block cowl and seams.

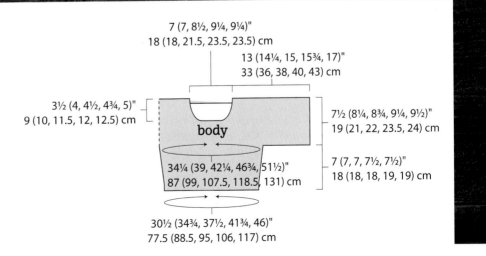

7 (7, 8½, 9¼, 9¼)"
18 (18, 21.5, 23.5, 23.5) cm

13 (14¼, 15, 15¾, 17)"
33 (36, 38, 40, 43) cm

3½ (4, 4½, 4¾, 5)"
9 (10, 11.5, 12, 12.5) cm

body

7½ (8¼, 8¾, 9¼, 9½)"
19 (21, 22, 23.5, 24) cm

34¼ (39, 42¼, 46¾, 51½)"
87 (99, 107.5, 118.5, 131) cm

7 (7, 7, 7½, 7½)"
18 (18, 18, 19, 19) cm

30½ (34¾, 37½, 41¾, 46)"
77.5 (88.5, 95, 106, 117) cm

Right Round MITTS

These quick to knit mitts spin right, and left, around your arms and hands. The lace repeat is easy to memorize and mirrored; the right mitt spins right and the left mitt spins left.

Finished Size
6" (15 cm) hand circumference.

Yarn
Fingering weight (#1 Super Fine)

Shown here: Tilli Tomas Artisan Sock (90% superwash Australian merino, 10% nylon; 440 yd [402 m]/100 g): atlantic, 1 hank.

Needles
Ribbing: U.S. size 1 (2.25 mm): set of 4 double-pointed (dpn).

Hand: U.S. size 2 (2.75 mm): set of 4 dpn.

Adjust needle size if necessary to obtain the correct gauge.

Notions
Markers (m); waste yarn; tapestry needle.

Gauge
34 sts and 48 rnds = 4" (10 cm) in Right Mitt chart on larger needles.

MELISSA GOODALE

NOTE

✪ Mitts are worked in the round on double-pointed needles.

Right Mitt

CUFF

Using smaller dpn, CO 56 sts. Place marker (pm) and join for working in the round, being careful not to twist sts.

Rnd 1: P1, k2, p1, *k1, [p2, k2] 3 times; rep from * to end.

Rep Rnd 1 six more times.

WRIST

Change to larger needles.

Set-up rnd: P1, k2, p1, pm, work Right Mitt chart to end.

Cont as established, work Rnds 1–6 of chart five times, then Rnd 1 once.

THUMB GUSSET

Inc rnd: P1, RLI (see Techniques), knit to 1 st before m, LLI (see Techniques), p1, sl m, work in patt to end—2 sts inc'd.

Next rnd: P1, knit to 1 st before m, p1, sl m, work in patt to end.

Rep the last 2 rnds ten more times—78 sts.

Next rnd: Place first 26 sts of rnd on waste yarn for thumb, remove m, work in patt to end—52 sts rem.

HAND

Work even for 18 rnds, ending with Rnd 6 of chart.

RIBBING

Change to smaller needles.

Next rnd: *K1, [p2, k2] 3 times; rep from * to end.

Rep last rnd six more times.

BO all sts using the sewn bind-off (see Techniques).

THUMB

Place 26 held sts on larger dpn. Join yarn.

Rnd 1: P1, knit to last st, p1.

Rnd 2: K2tog, knit to last 2 sts, ssk—24 sts.

Knit 4 rnds.

Work in k2, p2 rib for 6 rnds.

BO all sts using the sewn bind-off.

Left Mitt

CUFF

Using smaller dpn, CO 56 sts. Place marker (pm) and join for working in the round, being careful not to twist sts.

Rnd 1: P1, k2, p1, *[p2, k2] 3 times, k1; rep from * to end.

Rep Rnd 1 six more times.

WRIST

Change to larger needles.

Set-up rnd: P1, k2, p1, pm, work Left Mitt chart to end.

Cont as established, work Rnds 1–6 of chart five times, then Rnd 1 once.

THUMB GUSSET

Work as for right mitt.

HAND

Work as for right mitt.

RIBBING

Change to smaller needles.

Next rnd: *[K2, p2] 3 times, k1; rep from * around.

Rep last rnd six more times.

BO all sts using the sewn bind-off (see Techniques).

THUMB

Work as for right mitt.

Finishing

Weave in ends. Block.

Key

☐	k
⦁	p
○	yo
╱	k2tog
╲	ssk
☐	pattern repeat

Right Mitt

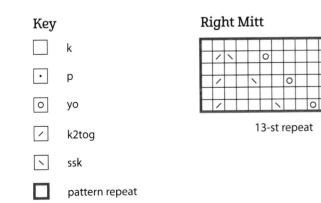

13-st repeat

Left Mitt

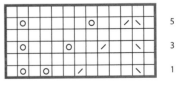

13-st repeat

Delancey COWL

This two-color cowl lets you experiment with color. Try two shades of the same color for a more subtle look, or go boldly graphic with lots of contrast. Have fun selecting buttons to add even more interest to your project!

Finished Size
About 25¼ (47)" (64 [119.5] cm) in circumference and 10¼" (26 cm) tall.

Yarn
Lace weight (#1 Super Fine)

Shown here: Ella Rae Lace Merino (100% superwash merino wool; 460 yd [421 m]/100 g): #41 chocolate (MC), 1 hank; #19 cream (CC), 1 hank.

Needles
U.S. size 6 (4 mm): 32" (80 cm) circular (cir).

Notions
Tapestry needle; ten ½" (12 mm) buttons.

Gauge
24 sts and 40 rows = 4" (10 cm) in garter st.

Adjust needle size if necessary to obtain the correct gauge.

KIRSTEN KAPUR

NOTES

✪ The openwork dot border is worked first, side to side. A circular needle is used to accommodate the large number of stitches. Additional stitches are then cast on for the striped portion, which is joined to the border with a decrease on every other row. The button bands are worked last.

✪ Take care to carry the yarn loosely behind the slipped stitches.

✪ When working the openwork dot border, do not cut yarns at color changes. Carry other yarn loosely up side of work until it is needed again. When working the striped portion, cut the yarns between color changes.

Purled Cast-On

*Purl into the first st on the left needle but do not drop the st. Place the st just made onto the left needle—1 st CO. Rep from * until desired number of sts have been cast on.

Cowl

OPENWORK DOT BORDER

Using the long-tail method and MC, CO 124 (232) sts. Do not join.

Knit 3 rows.

Work openwork dot patt:

Row 1: (RS) With MC, knit.

Row 2: With MC, purl.

Row 3: With CC, k1, *sl 2 pwise with yarn in back (wyb), k4; rep from * to last 3 sts, sl 2 pwise wyb, k1.

Row 4: With CC, k1, *sl 2 pwise with yarn in front (wyf), k4; rep from * to last 3 sts, sl 2 pwise wyf, k1.

Row 5: With CC, k1, *sl 2 pwise wyb, ssk, [yo] 2 times, k2tog; rep from * to last 3 sts, sl 2 pwise wyb, k1.

Row 6: With CC, k1, *sl 2 pwise wyf, k1, [k1, p1] into double yo, k1; rep from * to last 3 sts, sl 2 pwise wyf, k1.

Rows 7-10: Rep Rows 1 and 2 two times.

Row 11: With CC, k4, *sl 2 pwise wyb, k4; rep from * to end.

Row 12: With CC, k4, *sl 2 pwise wyf, k4; rep from * to end.

Row 13: With CC, k4, *sl 2 pwise wyb, ssk, [yo] 2 times, k2tog; rep from * to last 6 sts, sl 2 pwise wyb, k4.

Row 14: With CC, k4, *sl 2 pwise wyf, k1, [k1, p1] into double yo, k1; rep from * to last 6 sts, sl 2 pwise wyf, k4.

Rows 15-16: Rep Rows 1 and 2.

Rep Rows 1-16 once more, then Rows 1-8 once. Work measures about 4¼" (11 cm) from CO. Cut CC, do not cut MC.

STRIPED SECTION

With RS facing, using MC and the purled cast-on (see Stitch Guide), CO 36 sts—160 (268) sts.

Row 1: (RS) K35, k2tog (last st of striped section tog with 1 st from openwork dot border), turn—1 st dec'd.

Row 2: K36.

Rep Rows 1-2 seven more times—152 (260) sts rem.

Change to CC. Work Rows 1-2 six times—6 sts dec'd.

Change to MC. Work Rows 1-2 six times—6 sts dec'd.

Rep the last 24 rows 8 (17) more times—44 sts rem.

Change to CC. Work Rows 1-2 eight times—36 sts rem.

BO rem sts.

Finishing

Button band: With RS facing and using MC, pick up and knit 59 sts from short end of piece. Knit 9 rows. BO.

Buttonhole band: With RS facing and using MC, pick up and knit 59 sts from opposite short end of piece. Knit 3 rows.

Buttonhole row: (RS) K2, [yo, k2tog, k4] 9 times, yo, k2tog, k1.

Knit 5 rows. BO.

Weave in ends. Sew on buttons. Block.

Jujube HAT

When working this lace pattern you'll immediately be reminded of the jujube —a nutritious, snackable Asian stone fruit. The Jujube Hat combines a delicate stitch pattern with a feminine, folded picot brim and the perfect amount of slouch for a versatile hat that is wearable and fun to knit!

CARINA SPENCER

Finished Size
20¾" (52.5 cm) circumference

Yarn
Sport weight (#2 Fine)

Shown here: Alchemy Yarns of Transformation Temple (100% superfine merino wool; 128 yd [117 ml]/50 g): #198C dude ranch, 2 hanks.

Needles
U.S. size 4 (3.5 mm): 16" circular (cir) and set of 4 double-pointed (dpn).

Adjust needle size if necessary to obtain the correct gauge.

Notions
Waste yarn; spare 16" (40 cm) cir needle for hem, U.S. size 4 (3.5 mm) or smaller; marker (m); tapestry needle.

Gauge
23 sts and 34 rows = 4" (10 cm) in Jujube patt from chart.

Hat

HEMMED BRIM

Using the invisible provisional method (see Techniques) and cir needle, CO 100 sts. Place marker (pm) and join for working in the round, being careful not to twist sts. Knit 7 rnds.

Eyelet rnd: *Yo, k2tog; rep from * to end.

Knit 7 rnds.

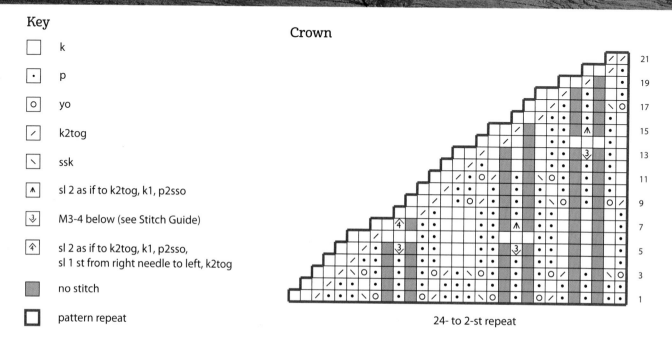

Key

☐	k
⊡	p
▢○	yo
⟋	k2tog
⟍	ssk
⋀	sl 2 as if to k2tog, k1, p2sso
⬇	M3-4 below (see Stitch Guide)
⬆	sl 2 as if to k2tog, k1, p2sso, sl 1 st from right needle to left, k2tog
▨	no stitch
☐	pattern repeat

Crown

24- to 2-st repeat

Remove waste yarn from provisional CO and place the resulting 100 live sts on spare cir needle. Fold work on eyelet rnd with wrong sides facing, holding the spare needle behind the working needle.

Joining rnd: *Insert right needle into first st on working needle, then first st on spare needle and knit them together as one st; rep from * to end.

Body

Next rnd: *K5, M1 (see Techniques); rep from * to end—120 sts.

Set-up rnd: *P2, k3, p3; rep from * to end.

Work Rnds 1–16 of Jujube chart 2 times, then Rnds 1–8 once. Hat measures about 5½" (14 cm) from folded edge.

Crown

Note: Change to dpns when there are too few sts to work comfortably on cir needle.

Shift beg of rnd as foll: Remove m, k1, pm for new beg of rnd.

Work Rnds 1–21 of Crown chart—10 sts rem. Break yarn, leaving a 6" (15 cm) tail. Thread tail onto tapestry needle and draw through rem sts, pull snug to tighten, and fasten off inside.

Finishing

Weave in ends. Block.

Jujube

15
13
11
9
7
5
3
1

8-st repeat

Essex Lace CAMISOLE

Just because you only have a few skeins of yarn, that doesn't mean you only have to make accessories. A simple lace pattern mixed with a lovely hand-dyed yarn makes this lace camisole an ideal addition to any wardrobe. The great thing about this style is the lace panel along the sides, which gives the illusion of shaping but eliminates the need to do any intricate shaping in the pattern.

Finished Size

29¼ (31½, 33½, 36½, 39½, 42¼)" (74.5 [80, 85, 92.5, 100.5, 107.5] cm) bust circumference.

Cami shown measures 31½" (80 cm).

Yarn

Fingering weight (#1 Super Fine)

Shown here: Neighborhood Fiber Co. Fingering (100% superwash merino; 475 yd [434 ml/113 g]): woodberry, 2 (2, 2, 2, 3, 3) hanks.

Needles

U.S. size 3 (3.25 mm): 24" (60 cm) circular (cir).

Adjust needle size if necessary to obtain the correct gauge.

Notions

Markers (m); stitch holders; tapestry needle.

Gauge

22 sts and 42 rows = 4" (10 cm) in trellis lace st; 26-st Sunray Lace panel measures 4¼" (11 cm) wide.

SAUNIELL CONNALLY

NOTES

✪ Camisole is worked in the round from the bottom up. Back and front are divided at armholes and worked separately, back-and-forth. The neck is shaped with short-rows. Do not wrap stitches when turning short-rows.

✪ During shaping, if there are not enough stitches to work each decrease with its companion yarnover, work the remaining stitch(es) in stockinette instead.

Trellis Lace Stitch in rnds (multiple of 2 sts + 1)

Rnd 1: K1, *yo, k2tog; rep from * to end.

Rnd 2: Knit.

Rnd 3: *Ssk, yo; rep from * to last st, k1.

Rnd 4: Knit.

Rep Rnds 1–4 for patt.

Trellis Lace Stitch in rows (multiple of 2 sts + 1)

Row 1: (RS) K1, *yo, k2tog; rep from * to end.

Row 2: Purl.

Row 3: *Ssk, yo; rep from * to last st, k1.

Row 4: Purl.

Rep Rows 1–4 for patt.

Camisole

CO 166 (178, 190, 206, 222, 238) sts, place marker (pm) and join to work in the round, taking care not to twist sts.

Knit 1 rnd. Purl 1 rnd.

Next rnd: *K2tog, yo; rep from * to end.

Knit 1 rnd. Purl 1 rnd.

Set-up rnd: K26, pm, k57 (63, 69, 77, 85, 93), pm, k26, pm, knit to end.

Next rnd: [Work Sunray Lace chart over 26 sts, sl m, work trellis lace st worked in rnds to next m, sl m] 2 times.

Cont in patt until piece measures about 16 (16, 16¼, 16½, 16¾, 17)" (40.5 [40.5, 41.5, 42, 42.5, 43] cm) from CO, ending with Rnd 2 or 4 of trellis lace patt.

Note: For most accurate results, lightly block the work before measuring.

Divide front and back: Work 13 sts in patt, BO 7 (8, 8, 8, 10, 12) sts, k1, work in patt to opposite side panel, sl m, work 13 sts in patt, place next 83 (89, 95, 103, 111, 119) sts on holder for back, turn to begin working back and forth in rows—76 (81, 87, 95, 101, 107) sts rem for front.

Upper Front

Next row: (WS) BO 7 (8, 8, 8, 10, 12) sts, k1, work in patt to last 2 sts, k2—69 (73, 79, 87, 91, 95) sts rem.

Dec row: (RS) K2, sl 1, k2tog, psso, work in patt to last 5 sts, k3tog, k2—4 sts dec'd.

Dec row: (WS) K2, p2tog tbl, work in patt to last 4 sts, p2tog, k2—2 sts dec'd.

Rep the last 2 rows 1 (1, 2, 3, 3, 3) more times, then RS dec row only 1 time—53 (57, 57, 59, 63, 67) sts rem.

Sizes 29¼ (31½)" (74.5 [80] cm) only:

Next row: (WS) K2, work in patt to last 2 sts, k2.

Dec row: K2, ssk, work in patt to last 4 sts, k2tog, k2—2 sts dec'd.

Rep the last 2 rows 0 (1) more time—51 (53) sts rem.

All sizes:

Work even, keeping 2 sts at each end in garter st, for 7 (7, 11, 11, 11, 13) rows, ending with a WS row.

Next row: (RS) Work 15 sts in patt, place next 21 (23, 27, 29, 33, 37) sts on a holder for neck, place rem 15 sts on a separate holder for right side—15 sts rem for left side. Turn.

Left side:

Next row: (WS) Work in patt to end.

Begin short-row shaping:

Short-row 1: (RS) Work 12 sts in patt, turn, do not wrap (see Notes).

Short-rows 2, 4, 6: (WS) Work in patt to end.

Short-row 3: Work 9 sts in patt, turn.

Short-row 5: Work 6 sts in patt, turn.

Short-row 7: Work 3 sts in patt, turn.

Short-row 8: (WS) Work in patt to end.

Place all sts on holder.

Right side:

Place 15 held right side sts on needle and join yarn with RS facing.

Next row: (RS) Work in patt to end.

Begin short-row shaping:

Short-row 1: (WS) Work 12 sts in patt, turn.

Short-rows 2, 4, 6: (RS) Work in patt to end.

Short-row 3: Work 9 sts in patt, turn.

Short-row 5: Work 6 sts in patt, turn.

Short-row 7: Work 3 sts in patt, turn.

Key

- ☐ k
- · p
- ⟋ k2tog
- ⟍ ssk
- ○ yo
- ⟋ k3tog
- ⟑ sl 1, k2tog, psso

Sunray Lace

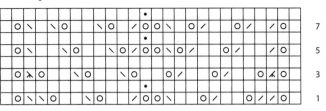

26 sts

Short-row 8: (RS) Work in patt to end.

Leave sts on needle. Do not break yarn.

Next row: (WS) K15 right side sts, k21 (23, 27, 29, 33, 37) held neck sts, k15 held left side sts—51 (53, 57, 59, 63, 67) sts.

Dec row: (RS) K2, k2tog, knit to last 4 sts, ssk, k2—2 sts dec'd.

Knit 1 row.

Rep Dec row—47 (49, 53, 55, 59, 63) sts rem.

Next row (WS): K3, BO 41 (43, 47, 49, 53, 57) sts, knit to end—3 sts rem each side. Place sts on holders.

Upper Back

Place 83 (89, 95, 103, 111, 119) held back sts on needle and join yarn with RS facing.

Next row: (RS) BO 4 (5, 5, 5, 7, 9) sts, k1, work in patt to end—79 (84, 90, 98, 104, 110) sts rem.

Next row: (WS) BO 4 (5, 5, 5, 7, 9) sts, k1, work in patt to last 2 sts, k2—75 (79, 85, 93, 97, 101) sts rem.

Dec row: (RS) K2, sl 1, k1, psso, work in patt to last 5 sts, k3tog, k2—4 sts dec'd.

Dec row: (WS) K2, p2tog tbl, work in patt to last 4 sts, p2tog, k2—2 sts dec'd.

Rep the last 2 rows 1 (1, 2, 3, 3, 3) more times, then RS dec row only 1 time—59 (63, 63, 65, 69, 73) sts rem.

Sizes 29¼ (31½)" (74.5 [80] cm) only:

Next row: (WS) K2, work in patt to last 2 sts, k2.

Dec row: K2, ssk, work in patt to last 4 sts, k2tog, k2—2 sts dec'd.

Rep the last 2 rows 0 (1) more time—57 (59) sts rem.

All sizes:

Work even, keeping 2 sts at each end in garter st, for 3 (3, 7, 7, 7, 9) rows, ending with a WS row.

Next row: (RS) Work 15 sts in patt, place next 27 (29, 33, 35, 39, 43) sts on a holder for neck, place rem 15 sts on a separate holder for left side—15 sts rem for right side. Turn.

Right side:

Next row: (WS) Work in patt to end.

Begin short-row shaping:

Short-row 1: (RS) Work 12 sts in patt, turn, do not wrap.

Short-rows 2, 4, 6: (WS) Work in patt to end.

Short-row 3: Work 9 sts in patt, turn.

Short-row 5: Work 6 sts in patt, turn.

Short-row 7: Work 3 sts in patt, turn.

Short-row 8: (WS) Work in patt to end.

Place all sts on holder.

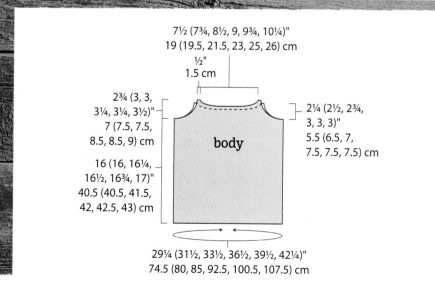

7½ (7¾, 8½, 9, 9¾, 10¼)"
19 (19.5, 21.5, 23, 25, 26) cm

½"
1.5 cm

2¾ (3, 3, 3¼, 3¼, 3½)"
7 (7.5, 7.5, 8.5, 8.5, 9) cm

2¼ (2½, 2¾, 3, 3, 3)"
5.5 (6.5, 7, 7.5, 7.5, 7.5) cm

16 (16, 16¼, 16½, 16¾, 17)"
40.5 (40.5, 41.5, 42, 42.5, 43) cm

body

29¼ (31½, 33½, 36½, 39½, 42¼)"
74.5 (80, 85, 92.5, 100.5, 107.5) cm

Left side:

Place 15 held left side sts on needle and join yarn with RS facing.

Next row: (RS) Work in patt to end.

Begin short-row shaping:

Short-row 1: (WS) Work 12 sts in patt, turn.

Short-rows 2, 4, 6: (RS) Work in patt to end.

Short-row 3: Work 9 sts in patt, turn.

Short-row 5: Work 6 sts in patt, turn.

Short-row 7: Work 3 sts in patt, turn.

Short-row 8: (RS) Work in patt to end.

Leave sts on needle. Do not break yarn.

Straps

Next row: (WS) K15 left side sts, k27 (29, 33, 35, 39, 43) held neck sts, k15 held right side sts—57 (59, 63, 65, 69, 73) sts.

Dec row: (RS) K2, k2tog, knit to last 4 sts, ssk, k2—2 sts dec'd.

Knit 1 row.

Rep Dec row—53 (55, 59, 61, 65, 69) sts rem.

Next row: (WS) K3, join a second ball of yarn and BO 47 (49, 53, 55, 59, 63) sts, knit to end—3 sts rem for each strap.

Working both straps at the same time with separate balls of yarn, work in garter st until straps measure 9 (9, 9.5, 9.5, 10, 10)" (23 [23, 24, 24, 25.5, 25.5] cm) from neck BO. Place sts on holders.

Finishing

Block to schematic measurements. Try on and adjust strap length to fit. Graft straps to front sts from holders. Weave in ends.

Yorkshire Morning MITTS

When the sun shines in Yorkshire, United Kingdom, it becomes one of the most beautiful places in the world. Since the weather can change in a moment, fingerless gloves are the perfect year-round accessory. The cable and lace panel along the top add interest for seasoned knitters and practice for newer knitters, without being fiddly. They're the perfect choice to show off a beautiful skein of solid luxury or hand-dyed yarn.

Finished Size
6¼ (7¼)" (16 [18.5]) cm in circumference and 9 (10½)" (23 [26.5] cm) long.

Mitts shown measure 6¼" (16 cm).

Yarn
DK weight (#3 Light)

Shown here: Rowan Pure Wool DK (100% superwash wool; 142 yd [130 m]/50 g): #048 clay, 1 (2) balls.

Needles
U.S. size 3 (3.25 mm): set of 4 double-pointed (dpn).

Adjust needle size if necessary to obtain the correct gauge.

Notions
Cable needle (cn); markers (m); waste yarn; tapestry needle.

Gauge
24 sts and 34 rows = 4" (10 cm) in St st.

KELLY HERDRICH

NOTE
✪ Mitts are worked in the round.

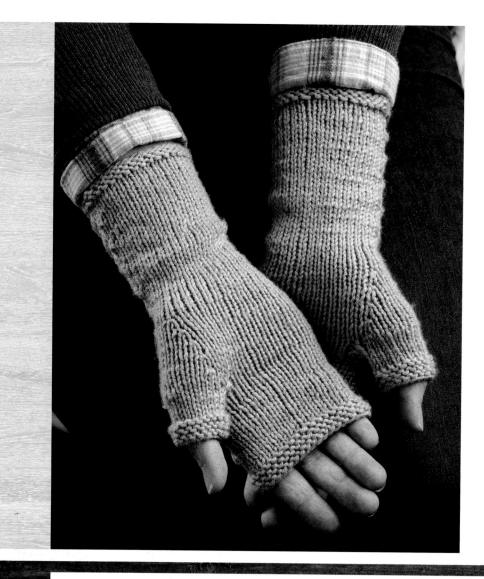

Right Mitt

WRIST

CO 37 (43) sts. Place marker (pm) and join for working in the round, being careful not to twist sts. Work in garter st (purl 1 rnd, knit 1 rnd) for 5 rnds. Change to St st and work 4 rnds even.

Set-up rnd: Work Yorkshire Cable chart over 17 sts, pm, knit to end.

Cont as established, work Rnds 1–6 of chart 6 (7) times.

THUMB GUSSET

Rnd 1: Work in patt to m, sl m, k1, pm for gusset, k1f&b (see Techniques), k1, k1f&b, pm for gusset, knit to end—39 (45) sts; 5 sts between gusset m.

Rnds 2–3: Work even.

Rnd 4: Work to gusset m, sl m, k1f&b, knit to 1 st before next m, k1f&b, sl m, knit to end—2 sts inc'd between gusset m.

Rep Rnds 2–4 four (five) more times—49 (57) sts; 15 (17) sts between gusset m.

Work 2 rnds even.

Next rnd: Work in patt to gusset m, remove m, place next 15 (17) sts on

Key

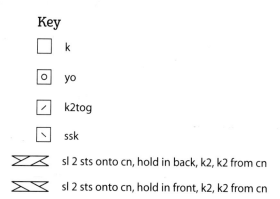

	k
	yo
	k2tog
	ssk
	sl 2 sts onto cn, hold in back, k2, k2 from cn
	sl 2 sts onto cn, hold in front, k2, k2 from cn

Yorkshire Cable

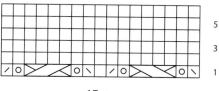

5

3

1

17 sts

waste yarn for thumb, remove m, use the backward loop method to CO 3 sts, knit to end—37 (43) sts rem.

HAND

Work even until you have completed a total of 11 (13) reps of chart, ending with Rnd 6.

Beg with a purl rnd, work in garter st for 5 rnds.

Loosely BO all sts.

THUMB

Place 15 (17) held sts on needle. Join yarn, pick up and knit 3 sts from CO edge, pm and join to work in the round—18 (20) sts.

Knit 6 rnds. Beg with a purl rnd, work in garter st for 5 rnds.

Loosely BO all sts.

Left Mitt

WRIST

Work as for right mitt.

THUMB GUSSET

Rnd 1: Work in patt to last 4 sts, pm for gusset, k1f&b, k1, k1f&b, pm for gusset, k1—39 (45) sts; 5 sts between gusset m.

Complete as for right mitt.

Finishing

Weave in ends. Block.

Clifton SHAWL

This shawl is a light and airy crescent shape worked in one hank of luxurious laceweight yarn. The shawl is worked from the bottom up, beginning with an intriguing lace pattern with mock cables. The body is worked in stockinette stitch, with short-rows shaping the shawl. The top edge uses the same mock cable as the bottom edge; however, a full repeat of the mock cable pattern is not worked, creating an interesting slipped stitch ribbing.

Finished Size
About 57¼" (145.5 cm) wide and 6" (15 cm) deep

Yarn
Lace weight (#1 Super Fine)

Shown here: Swans Island Merino Silk Lace (50% fine merino wool, 50% tussah silk; 530 yd [485 ml]/50 g): currant, 1 hank.

Needles
Cast on: U.S. size 4 (3.5 mm): 40" (100 cm) circular (cir). Shawl: U.S. size 3 (3.25 mm): 40" (100 cm) cir.

Adjust needle size if necessary to obtain the correct gauge.

Notions
Tapestry needle.

Gauge
21 sts and 38 rows = 4" (10 cm) in St st on smaller needle.

MINDY WILKES

NOTES

✪ Shawl is worked flat. Circular needles are used to accommodate the large number of stitches.

✪ Shawl is worked from the bottom up. Short-rows are used to create the crescent shape. Do not wrap stitches when turning short-rows.

Shawl

Using larger needle and the knitted CO method (see Techniques), CO 365 sts. Do not join. Change to smaller needle.

Bottom Edging

Row 1: (WS) K1, p3, k1, *p2, k1, [p3, k1] twice, p2, k1, p3, k1; rep from * to end.

Row 2: *P1, k3, p1, k2, [p1, k3] twice, p1, k2; rep from * to last 5 sts, p1, k3, p1.

Rep Rows 1–2 two more times, then Row 1 once.

Work Rows 1–4 of Edging chart two times, then Rows 5–12 three times, then Rows 13–14 once—325 sts rem.

Body

Shape shawl using short-rows as foll:

Short-row 1: (RS) K241, turn, do not wrap (see Notes).

Short-row 2: (WS) P157, turn.

Short-row 3: Knit to 1 st before previous turn, ssk, k6, turn —1 st dec'd.

Short-row 4: Purl to 1 st before previous turn, p2tog, p6, turn —1 st dec'd.

Rep Short-rows 3–4 eleven more times—301 sts rem.

Top Edging

Row 1: (RS) *P1, mock cable (see Stitch Guide); rep from * to last st, p1.

Row 2: K1, *p3, k1; rep from * to end.

Loosely BO all sts in patt.

Finishing

Weave in ends. Block to measurements, shaping into a crescent.

Key

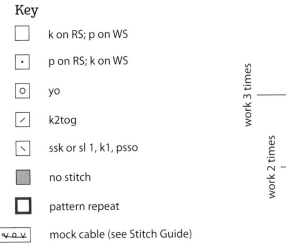

☐   k on RS; p on WS

·   p on RS; k on WS

○   yo

╱   k2tog

╲   ssk or sl 1, k1, psso

▨   no stitch

☐   pattern repeat

⎯   mock cable (see Stitch Guide)

Edging

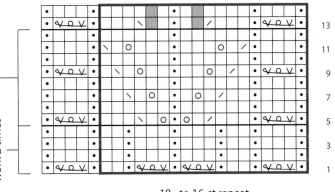

18- to 16-st repeat

Quinsnicket COWL

Quinsnicket is an homage to the stark beauty of trees. Simple cables and easy texture are tweaked—the cable is ribbed, rendering it reversible, and the slipped-stitch edge keeps things looking neat from all angles.

Finished Size
8" (20.5 cm) wide and 89" (226 cm) in circumference.

Yarn
Aran weight (#4 Medium)

Shown here: Schoppel Wolle In-Silk (75% merino wool, 25% silk; 219 yd [200 m]/100g): #8495 80% cocoa, 3 hanks

Needles
U.S. size 10¾ (7 mm): straight.

Adjust needle size if necessary to obtain the correct gauge.

Notions
Cable needle (cn); tapestry needle.

Gauge
38 sts = 8" (20.5 cm) and 18 rows = 4" (10 cm) in cable patt from chart.

CIRILIA ROSE

NOTE

✪ Cowl is worked back and forth as a long strip, then sewn into a loop.

Cowl

CO 38 sts. Purl 1 row **(WS)**. Rep Rows 1–8 of Cable chart until cowl measures about 89" (226 cm) from CO, ending with Row 8. BO all sts.

Finishing

Seam CO and BO edges together. Weave in ends. Block.

Key

☐	k on RS; p on WS
·	p on RS; k on WS
o	yo
∕	p2tog on WS
∕	p2tog on RS
v	sl 1 wyb

sl 4 to cn, hold to front, [k1, p1] 2 times, [k1, p1] 2 times from cn

sl 4 to cn, hold to back, [k1, p1] 2 times, [k1, p1] 2 times from cn

Cable

38 sts

Foliage HAT AND MITTS

The leaf motif in this hat and mitts is used like one would use a cable pattern; traditional shapes are given a subtle twist with the leaf growing over the edge. The construction of the hat, knit from the top down, was dictated by the design.

Finished Size
Hat: About 17" (43 cm) circumference.

Mitts: About 6" (15 cm) circumference.

Yarn
DK weight (#3 Light)

Shown here: Dragonfly Fibers Traveller (100% superwash merino; 280 yd [256 m]/113 g): Spanish moss, 1 hank.

Needles
U.S. size 7 (4.5 mm): 16" (40 cm) circular (cir) and set of 4 double-pointed (dpn).

Adjust needle size if necessary to obtain the correct gauge.

Notions
Markers (m); cable needle (cn); tapestry needle.

Gauge
24 sts and 26 rows = 4" (10 cm) in relaxed k1, p1 rib.

ERICA SCHLUETER

NOTES

✪ Hat is worked in the round from the top down.

✪ Mitts are worked in the round from the wrist up.

P1f&b

purl into front, then back of same st—1 st inc'd.

S2kp2

sl 2 as if to k2tog, k1, pass 2 sl sts over knit st—2 sts dec'd.

Rnd 6: [K1, M1P, p1] 2 times, k1, sl m, work Rnd 6 of chart, sl m, [k1, M1P, p1] 4 times—30 sts.

Rnd 7: [K1, p2] 2 times, k1, sl m, work Rnd 7 of chart, sl m, [k1, p2] 4 times.

Rnd 8: [K1, p1, M1L, p1] 2 times, k1, sl m, work Rnd 8 of chart, sl m, [k1, p1, M1L, p1] 4 times—38 sts.

Rnd 9: [K1, p1] 4 times, k1, sl m, work Rnd 9 of chart, sl m, [k1, p1] 8 times.

Rnd 10: [K1, M1P, p1] 4 times, k1, sl m, work Rnd 10 of chart, sl m, [k1, M1P, p1] 8 times—52 sts.

Rnd 11: [K1, p2] 4 times, k1, sl m, work Rnd 11 of chart, sl m, [k1, p2] 8 times.

Rnd 12: [K1, p2] 4 times, k1, work Rnd 12 of chart, sl m, [k1, p2] 8 times.

Rnd 13: [K1, p2] 4 times, k1, sl m, work Rnd 13 of chart, sl m, [k1, p2] 8 times—54 sts.

Rnd 14: [K1, p2] 4 times, k1, sl m, work Rnd 14 of chart, sl m, [k1, p2] 8 times.

Rnd 15: [K1, p1, M1L, p1] 4 times, k1, sl m, work Rnd 15 of chart, sl m, [k1, p1, M1L, p1] 8 times—68 sts.

Rnd 16: [K1, p1] 8 times, k1, sl m, work Rnd 16 of chart, sl m, [k1, p1] 16 times.

Rnd 17: [K1, p1] 8 times, k1, sl m, work Rnd 17 of chart, sl m, [k1, p1] 16 times—70 sts.

Hat

CROWN

With dpn, CO 6 sts. Place marker (pm) and join to work in the round, taking care not to twist sts.

Set-up rnd: [K1, use the backward-loop method (see Techniques) to CO 1 st] 5 times, k1—11 sts.

Rnd 1: K1, p1, k1, pm, work Rnd 1 of Hat chart over 4 sts, pm, [k1, p1] 2 times—12 sts.

Rnd 2: K1, M1P (see Techniques), p1, k1, sl m, work Rnd 2 of chart, sl m, [k1, M1P, p1] 2 times—17 sts.

Rnd 3: K1, p2, k1, sl m, work Rnd 3 of chart, sl m, [k1, p2] 2 times.

Rnd 4: K1, p1, M1L (see Techniques), p1, k1, sl m, work Rnd 4 of chart, sl m, [k1, p1, M1L, p1] 2 times—22 sts.

Rnd 5: [K1, p1] 2 times, k1, sl m, work Rnd 5 of chart, sl m, [k1, p1] 4 times.

Key

□	k
·	p
℞	k1 tbl
▨	no stitch
╱	k2tog
╲	ssk
↗	p2tog
↖	p2tog tbl
⋏	sl 1, k2tog, psso
↓	p1f&b (see Stitch Guide)
ML	M1L
MP	M1 pwise
○	yo
▣	pattern repeat
⌣	[k1, yo, k1] in same st
◤◥ b	sl 1 st onto cn, hold in back, k1 tbl, p1 from cn
◢◣	sl 1 st onto cn, hold in front, p1, k1 tbl from cn
◢◣	sl 1 st onto cn, hold in front, p1f&b , k1 tbl from cn

Hat

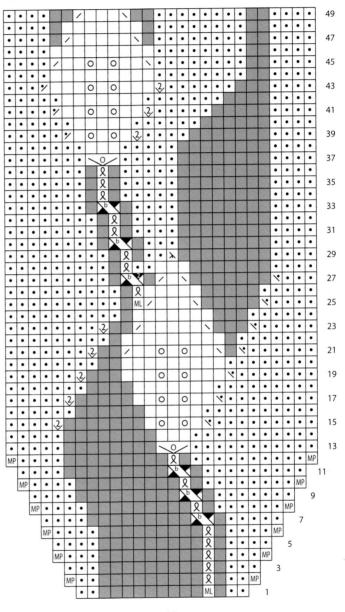

4 to 21 sts

Rnd 18: [K1, p1] 8 times, k1, sl m, work Rnd 18 of chart, sl m, [k1, p1] 16 times.

Rnd 19: [K1, p1] 8 times, k1, sl m, work Rnd 19 of chart, sl m, [k1, p1] 16 times—72 sts.

Rnd 20: [K1, p1] 3 times, k1, [M1P, p1, k1] 2 times, [p1, k1] 3 times, sl m, work Rnd 20 of chart, sl m, [k1, p1] 3 times, k1, [M1P, p1, k1] 2 times, [p1, k1] 5 times, [M1P, p1, k1] 4 times, p1, k1, p1—80 sts.

Change to cir needle.

Row 21: [K1, p1] 3 times, k1, [p1, M1L, p1, k1] 2 times, [p1, k1] 3 times, sl m, work Rnd 21 of chart, sl m, [k1, p1] 3 times, k1, [p1, M1L, p1, k1] 2 times, [p1, k1] 5 times, [p1, M1L, p1, k1] 4 times, p1, k1, p1—90 sts.

HAT BODY

Next rnd: *K1, p1; rep from * to 1 st before m, k1, sl m, work next rnd of chart, **k1, p1; rep from ** to end.

Cont in patt through Rnd 49 of chart—86 sts.

Next rnd: Work in patt to m, remove m, p12, k5, BO 81 sts in patt, removing m, sl 1 st from right needle to left, ssk, k1, k2tog—3 sts of leaf rem. Turn.

Next row : (WS) P3.

Next row: Sl 1, k2tog, psso—1 st rem.

Fasten off last st.

Key

☐	k
·	p
ℵ	k1 tbl
▓	no stitch
╱	k2tog
╲	ssk
⅄	p2tog
⅄	p2tog tbl
⋏	sl 1, k2tog, psso
⅄	p1f&b (see Stitch Guide)
ML	M1L
MP	M1 pwise
o	yo
☐	pattern repeat
⌣o	[k1, yo, k1] in same st
▚	sl 1 st onto cn, hold in back, k1 tbl, p1 from cn
▞	sl 1 st onto cn, hold in front, p1, k1 tbl from cn
▚ b	sl 1 st onto cn, hold in back, k1 tbl, p1f&b from cn
▞ b	sl 1 st onto cn, hold in front, p1f&b , k1 tbl from cn

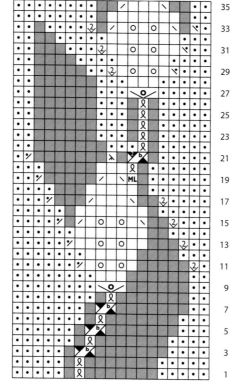

Left Mitt

11 to 15 sts

Right Mitt

11 to 15 sts

LEAF TOPPER

Stem:

CO 3 sts on one dpn. Work I-cord (see Techniques) for 7 rows.

Leaf:

Rows 1, 3, 5, 7, 9, 11, 13, 15 : (WS) Purl.

Row 2: (RS) K1, M1R (see Techniques), k1, M1L, k1—5 sts.

Row 4: K2, yo, k1, yo, k2—7 sts.

Row 6: K1, ssk, yo, k1, yo, k2tog, k1.

Row 8: K1, M1R, ssk, yo, k1, yo, k2tog, M1L, k1—9 sts.

Row 10: K1, ssk, k3, k2tog, k1—7 sts rem.

Row 12: K1, ssk, k1, k2tog, k1—5 sts rem.

Row 14: K1, s2kp2 (see Stitch Guide), k1—3 sts rem.

Row 16: S2kp2—1 st rem.

Fasten off last st.

Sew to top of hat. Weave in ends.

Right Mitt

With dpn, CO 32 sts. Pm and join to work in the round, taking care not to twist sts.

Set-up rnd: [K1, p1] 5 times, k1, pm, work Right Mitt chart over 11 sts, pm, [k1, p1] 5 times.

Cont in patt through Rnd 29 of chart—36 sts.

THUMB HOLE

Next rnd: Work in patt to m, sl m, work chart, sl m, k1, p1, BO 5 sts, work in patt to end.

Next rnd: Work in patt to BO sts, use the knitted method (see Techniques) to CO 5 sts, work in patt to end.

Cont in patt through Rnd 35 of chart—36 sts.

Next rnd: Work in patt to m, remove m, p8, k5, BO 31 sts in patt, removing m, sl 1 st from right needle to left, ssk, k1, k2tog—3 sts of leaf rem. Turn.

Next row: (WS) P3.

Next row: Sl 1, k2tog, psso—1 st rem.

Fasten off last st.

Left Mitt

With dpn, CO 32 sts. Pm and join to work in the round, taking care not to twist sts.

Set-up rnd: [K1, p1] 5 times, k1, pm, work Left Mitt chart over 11 sts, pm, [k1, p1] 5 times.

Cont in patt through Rnd 29 of chart—36 sts.

THUMB HOLE

Next rnd: [K1, p1] 2 times, BO 5 sts, work in patt to end.

Next rnd: Work in patt to BO sts, use the knitted method (see Techniques) to CO 5 sts, work in patt to end.

Cont in patt through Rnd 35 of chart—36 sts.

Next rnd: Work in patt to m, remove m, p2, k5, BO 31 sts in patt, removing m, sl 1 st from right needle to left, ssk, k1, k2tog—3 sts of leaf rem. Turn.

Next row: (WS) P3.

Next row: Sl 1, k2tog, psso—1 st rem.

Fasten off last st.

Finishing

Weave in ends. Block.

Carmilla SHAWL

1 SKEIN

Designed to make the most of the stunning silk yarn, this shawl features a deep border with beautiful lace motifs embellished with beads and nupps. The lace pattern is created with basic lace stitches; the beads and nupps are optional. The shawl is worked from the bottom lace edge and it is formed into a versatile crescent shape with short-rows. Finally, a scattering of beads is included for a little additional sparkle.

Finished Size
About 60" (152.5 cm) wingspan and 27" (68.5 cm) deep.

Yarn
Lace weight (#1 Super Fine)

Shown here: Handmaiden Fine Yarn Lace Silk (100% silk; 985 yd [900 m]/100 g): wine, 1 hank.

Needles
Cast-on: U.S. size 9 (5.5 mm): 32" (80 cm) circular (cir).

Shawl: U.S. size 6 (4 mm): 32" cir.

Bind-off: U.S. size 7 (4.5 mm): straight.

Adjust needle size if necessary to obtain the correct gauge.

Notions
725 size 8/0 seed beads; size 10 (1.3 mm) steel crochet hook; tapestry needle.

Gauge
24 sts and 32 rows = 4" (10 cm) in St st on smallest needle.

SUSANNA IC

NOTES

✪ Shawl is worked flat. Circular needles are used to accommodate the large number of stitches.

✪ Shawl is worked from the bottom up. Short-rows (see Techniques) are used to create the crescent shape. Do not wrap stitches when turning short-rows.

✪ A loose cast-on and firm (not tight) bind-off are essential: the cast-on to allow the points of the edging to be pinned out, and the bind-off to support the crescent shape of the shawl during blocking and allow the lace to stretch fully.

Stitch Guide

Place Bead

Slide bead onto crochet hook, insert crochet hook pwise into st and sl st onto crochet hook, slide bead down hook onto st, then return st to left needle and k1.

S2kp2

Sl 2 sts as if to k2tog, k1, pass 2 sl sts over knit st—2 sts dec'd.

Shawl

EDGING

With largest needle, loosely CO 399 sts. Change to smallest needle. Work Rows 1–60 of Lace chart—267 sts rem.

Shape crescent with short-rows as foll:

Set 1:

Short-row 1: (RS) P1, k11, [yo, s2kp2, yo, k9] ten times, yo, s2kp2, yo, k5, turn, do not wrap (see Notes).

Short-row 2: (WS) P13, turn.

Short-row 3: K5, yo, s2kp2, yo, k4, ssk, k3, yo, s2kp2, yo, k5, turn—266 sts rem.

Short-rows 4, 6, 8, 10, 12, 14, 16, 18, 20: (WS) Purl to 1 st before previous turn, p2tog, p11, turn—1 st dec'd.

Short-row 5: K5, [yo, s2kp2, yo, k8] two times, yo, s2kp2, yo, k4, ssk, k3, yo, s2kp2, yo, k5, turn—264 sts rem.

Short-row 7: K5, [yo, s2kp2, yo, k8] four times, yo, s2kp2, yo, k4, ssk, k3, yo, s2kp2, yo, k5, turn—262 sts rem.

Short-row 9: K5, [yo, s2kp2, yo, k8] six times, yo, s2kp2, yo, k4, ssk, k3, yo, s2kp2, yo, k5, turn—260 sts rem.

Short-row 11: K5, [yo, s2kp2, yo, k8] eight times, yo, s2kp2, yo, k4, ssk, k3, yo, s2kp2, yo, k5, turn—258 sts rem.

Short-row 13: K5, [yo, s2kp2, yo, k8]

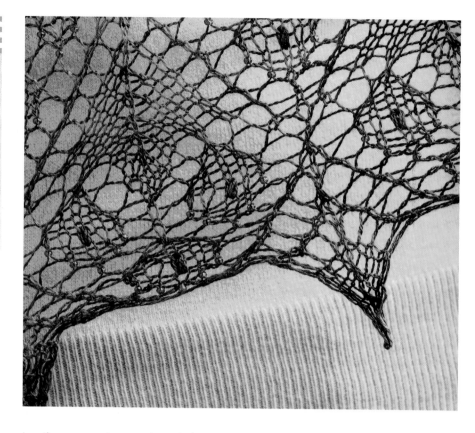

ten times, yo, s2kp2, yo, k4, ssk, k3, yo, s2kp2, yo, k5, turn—256 sts rem.

Short-row 15: K5, [yo, s2kp2, yo, k8] twelve times, yo, s2kp2, yo, k4, ssk, k3, yo, s2kp2, yo, k5, turn—254 sts rem.

Short-row 17: K5, [yo, s2kp2, yo, k8] fourteen times, yo, s2kp2, yo, k4, ssk, k3, yo, s2kp2, yo, k5, turn—252 sts rem.

Short-row 19: K5, [yo, s2kp2, yo, k8] sixteen times, yo, s2kp2, yo, k4, ssk, k3, yo, s2kp2, yo, k5, turn—250 sts rem.

Short-row 21: K5, [yo, s2kp2, yo, k8] eighteen times, yo, s2kp2, yo, k4, ssk, k3, yo, s2kp2, yo, k5, turn—248 sts rem.

Short-row 22: (WS) Purl to 1 st before previous turn, p2tog, p11, turn—247 sts rem.

Next row: (RS) K5, [yo, s2kp2, yo, k8] twenty times, yo, s2kp2, yo, k4, ssk, knit to last st, p1—246 sts rem.

Next row: (WS) Purl to 1 st before previous turn, p2tog, purl to end—245 sts rem.

Set 2:

Short-row 1: (RS) P1, k10, [yo, s2kp2, yo, k8] ten times, yo, s2kp2, yo, k4, turn.

Short-row 2: (WS) P11, turn.

Short-row 3: K4, yo, s2kp2, yo, k3, ssk, k3, yo, s2kp2, yo, k4, turn—244 sts rem.

Short-rows 4, 6, 8, 10, 12, 14, 16, 18, 20: (WS) Purl to 1 st before previous turn, p2tog, p10, turn—1 st dec'd.

Short-row 5: K4, [yo, s2kp2, yo, k7] two times, yo, s2kp2, yo, k3, ssk, k3, yo, s2kp2, yo, k4, turn—242 sts rem.

Short-row 7: K4, [yo, s2kp2, yo, k7] four times, yo, s2kp2, yo, k3, ssk, k3, yo, s2kp2, yo, k4, turn—240 sts rem.

Short-row 9: K4, [yo, s2kp2, yo, k7] six times, yo, s2kp2, yo, k3, ssk, k3, yo, s2kp2, yo, k4, turn—238 sts rem.

Short-row 11: K4, [yo, s2kp2, yo, k7] eight times, yo, s2kp2, yo, k3, ssk, k3, yo, s2kp2, yo, k4, turn—236 sts rem.

Key

- ☐ k on RS; p on WS
- • p on RS; k on WS
- ▧ no stitch
- ○ yo
- ╱ k2tog
- ╲ ssk
- ∧ s2kp2 (see Stitch Guide)
- ⊎ nupp: (k1, yo, k1, yo, k1, yo, k1) in same st
- ⇧ p7tog
- ⬛ place bead
- ▢ pattern repeat

Lace

18- to 12-st repeat

Short-row 13: K4, [yo, s2kp2, yo, k7] ten times, yo, s2kp2, yo, k3, ssk, k3, yo, s2kp2, yo, k4, turn—234 sts rem.

Short-row 15: K4, [yo, s2kp2, yo, k7] twelve times, yo, s2kp2, yo, k3, ssk, k3, yo, s2kp2, yo, k4, turn—232 sts rem.

Short-row 17: K4, [yo, s2kp2, yo, k7] fourteen times, yo, s2kp2, yo, k3, ssk, k3, yo, s2kp2, yo, k4, turn—230 sts rem.

Short-row 19: K4, [yo, s2kp2, yo, k7] sixteen times, yo, s2kp2, yo, k3, ssk, k3, yo, s2kp2, yo, k4, turn—228 sts rem.

Short-row 21: K4, [yo, s2kp2, yo, k7] eighteen times, yo, s2kp2, yo, k3, ssk, k3, yo, s2kp2, yo, k4, turn—226 sts rem.

Short-row 22: (WS) Purl to 1 st before previous turn, p2tog, p10, turn—225 sts rem.

Next row: (RS) K4, [yo, s2kp2, yo, k7] twenty times, yo, s2kp2, yo, k3, ssk, knit to last st, p1—224 sts rem.

Next row: (WS) Purl to 1 st before previous turn, p2tog, purl to end—223 sts rem.

Set 3:

Short-row 1: (RS) P1, k9, [yo, s2kp2, yo, k7] ten times, yo, s2kp2, yo, k4, turn.

Short-row 2: (WS) P11, turn.

Short-row 3: K4, yo, s2kp2, yo, k3, ssk, k2, yo, s2kp2, yo, k4, turn—222 sts rem.

Short-rows 4, 6, 8, 10, 12, 14, 16, 18, 20: (WS) Purl to 1 st before previous turn, p2tog, p9, turn—1 st dec'd.

Short-row 5: K4, [yo, s2kp2, yo, k6] two times, yo, s2kp2, yo, k3, ssk, k2, yo, s2kp2, yo, k4, turn—220 sts rem.

Short-row 7: K4, [yo, s2kp2, yo, k6] four times, yo, s2kp2, yo, k3, ssk, k2, yo, s2kp2, yo, k4, turn—218 sts rem.

Short-row 9: K4, [yo, s2kp2, yo, k6] six times, yo, s2kp2, yo, k3, ssk, k2, yo, s2kp2, yo, k4, turn—216 sts rem.

Short-row 11: K4, [yo, s2kp2, yo, k6] eight times, yo, s2kp2, yo, k3, ssk, k2, yo, s2kp2, yo, k4, turn—214 sts rem.

Short-row 13: K4, [yo, s2kp2, yo, k6] ten times, yo, s2kp2, yo, k3, ssk, k2, yo, s2kp2, yo, k4, turn—212 sts rem.

Short-row 15: K4, [yo, s2kp2, yo, k6] twelve times, yo, s2kp2, yo, k3, ssk, k2, yo, s2kp2, yo, k4, turn—210 sts rem.

Short-row 17: K4, [yo, s2kp2, yo, k6] fourteen times, yo, s2kp2, yo, k3, ssk, k2, yo, s2kp2, yo, k4, turn—208 sts rem.

Short-row 19: K4, [yo, s2kp2, yo, k6] sixteen times, yo, s2kp2, yo, k3, ssk, k2, yo, s2kp2, yo, k4, turn—206 sts rem.

Short-row 21: K4, [yo, s2kp2, yo, k6] eighteen times, yo, s2kp2, yo, k3, ssk, k2, yo, s2kp2, yo, k4, turn—204 sts rem.

Short-row 22: (WS) Purl to 1 st before previous turn, p2tog, p9, turn—203 sts rem.

Next row: (RS) K4, [yo, s2kp2, yo, k6] twenty times, yo, s2kp2, yo, k3, ssk, knit to last st, p1—202 sts rem.

Next row: (WS) Purl to 1 st before previous turn, p2tog, purl to end—201 sts rem.

TOP EDGE

Purl 2 rows.

Next row: (RS) K10, *place bead, k8; rep from * to last 11 sts, place bead, k10.

Next row: Knit all sts tbl.

Change to size 7 (4.5 mm) needles.

BO all sts as foll: *P2tog, sl 1 st from right needle to left; rep from * until 1 st rem. Fasten off last st.

Finishing

Weave in ends. Block piece to measurements and crescent shape. Start with the two short sides followed by the lace center point, then pin out the rest of the points along the edge.

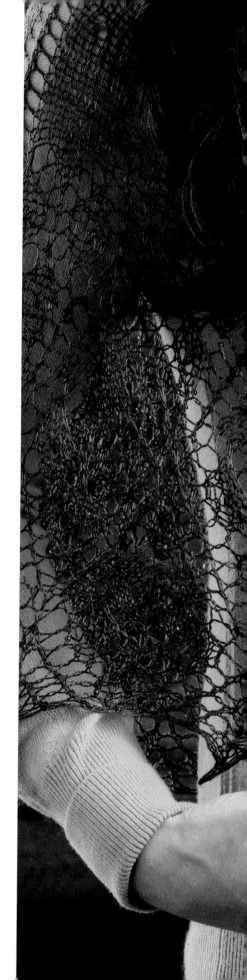

Ogival SOCKS

These socks were inspired by the gorgeous gothic cathedrals seen throughout Europe. One of the defining characteristics of Gothic architecture is the pointed or ogival arch, which is captured on the pattern of this sock.

Finished Size
About 7½" (19 cm) foot circumference.

Yarn
Super fine #1 (fingering weight)

Shown here: SweetGeorgia Yarns Tough Love Sock (80% superwash merino wool, 20% nylon; 425 yd [389 m]/115 g): hush, 1 hank.

Needles
U.S. size 1½ (2.5 mm): set of 4 double-pointed.

Adjust needle size if necessary to obtain the correct gauge.

Notions
Markers (m); tapestry needle.

Gauge
33 sts and 46 rnds = 4" (10 cm) in St st.

CARRIE SULLIVAN

NOTES

✪ Socks are worked from the cuff down.

✪ The cuff of this sock is patterned and may not provide as much stretch as a traditional ribbed cuff. Going up a needle size for the first 8–12 rounds will provide additional stretch if needed.

Key

☐	k
·	p
ℛ	k1 tbl
○	yo
╱	k2tog
╲	ssk
⅋	[sl 1 st kwise] 2 times, transfer both sts to left needle, k2tog
↘	k2tog tbl
☐	pattern repeat

Instep

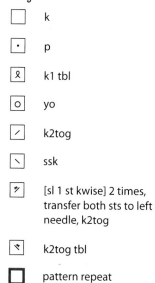

35 sts

Leg

17 sts

Leg

CO 68 sts, place marker (pm) and join to work in the round, taking care not to twist sts. Work Rnds 1–32 of Leg chart once, then Rnds 1–31 once.

Next rnd: Work Rnd 32 of chart to last st, turn, leaving last st unworked.

Heel Flap

Heel is worked over 33 sts.

Row 1: (WS) Sl 1, p32.

Row 2: (RS) [Sl 1 pwise with yarn in back (wyb), k1] 16 times, k1.

Rep Rows 1–2 nineteen more times, then Row 1 once. Heel flap measures about 2¼" (5.5 cm).

Turn Heel

Row 1: (RS) Sl 1, k17, ssk, k1, turn—1 st dec'd.

Row 2: (WS) Sl 1, p4, p2tog, p1, turn—1 st dec'd.

Row 3: Sl 1, knit to 1 st before previous turn, ssk, k1, turn—1 st dec'd.

Row 4: Sl 1, purl to 1 st before previous turn, p2tog, p1, turn—1 st dec'd.

Rep Rows 3–4 five more times—19 sts rem.

Gusset

Set-up rnd: K9, pm for new beg of rnd, k10, pick up and knit 21 sts along left edge of heel flap, pm for instep, work Rnd 1 of Instep chart over 35 sts, pm for instep, pick up and knit 21 sts along right edge of heel flap, knit to end—96 sts.

Rnd 1: Knit to instep m, sl m, work chart as established, sl m, knit to end.

Rnd 2: Knit to 3 sts before instep m, k2tog, k1, sl m, work chart as established, sl m, k1, ssk, knit to end—2 sts dec'd.

Rep Rnds 1–2 thirteen more times—68 sts rem; 35 sts for instep and 33 sts for sole.

Foot

Cont in patt through Rnd 49 of chart, then rep Rnd 49 until foot from back of heel measures 2" (5 cm) less than desired total length.

Toe

Set-up rnd: Knit to first instep m, remove m, k1, pm, knit to end—34 sts each for instep and sole.

Rnd 1: Knit.

Rnd 2: [Knit to 3 sts before m, k2tog, k1, sl m, k1, ssk] 2 times, knit to end—4 sts dec'd.

Rep Rnds 1–2 eight more times—32 sts rem. Rep Rnd 2 four times—16 sts rem.

Finishing

Graft toe closed using Kitchener st (see Techniques). Weave in ends. Block.

Mixed Berries HAT

This Fair Isle design features an unusual motif paired with textural and color choices that make the hat stand out, but remain easily knittable and wearable. Straight ribs in the brim flow directly up into a geometric colorwork motif. The crown shaping is clean and simple and gives the hat a classic fitted shape.

Finished Size
19¼ (21¼)" (49 [54] cm) in circumference. Hat shown measures 19¼" (49 cm).

Yarn
DK weight (#3 Light)

Shown here: Manos del Uruguay Silk Blend (70% extrafine merino wool, 30% silk; 150 yd [135 ml]/50 g): #300M bing cherry (dark purple) (MC), 1 hank; #3202 zinnia (orange) (CC1), 1 hank; #3082 shocking (pink) (CC2), 1 hank.

Needles
Brim: U.S. size 5 (3.5 mm) 16" (40 cm) circular (cir).

Body: U.S. size 6 (4 mm) 16" (40 cm) cir and set of 4 double-pointed (dpn).

Adjust needle size if necessary to obtain the correct gauge.

Notions
Markers (m); tapestry needle.

Gauge
22½ sts and 28 rows = 4" (10 cm) in St st on larger needle; 22½ sts and 24 rows = 4" (10 cm) in Mixed Berries chart on larger needle.

THEA COLMAN

NOTE
✪ Hat is worked in the round in stranded color work. Carry color not in use loosely across the WS of the work.

Brim

With MC and smaller cir needle, CO 108 (120) sts. Place marker (pm) and join to work in the round, being careful not to twist sts. Work in k1, p2 rib for 1¼" (3 cm). Change to larger cir needle.

Body

Work Rnds 1–21 of Mixed Berries chart. Continuing with MC only, knit 1 rnd. Hat measures about 5" (12.5 cm) from CO.

Crown

Note: Change to dpn when there are too few sts to work comfortably on cir needle.

Set-up rnd: *K12, pm; rep from * to end.

Dec rnd: *K2tog, knit to 2 sts before m, ssk, sl m; rep from * to end—18 (20) sts dec'd.

Knit 4 rnds. Rep Dec rnd—72 (80) sts rem.

Knit 3 rnds. Rep Dec rnd—54 (60) sts rem.

Knit 2 rnds. Rep Dec rnd—36 (40) sts rem.

Knit 1 rnd. Rep Dec rnd—18 (20) sts rem.

Size 19¼" (49 cm) only:

Next rnd: *K2tog, ssk; rep from * to last 2 sts, k2tog—9 sts rem.

Size 21¼" (54 cm) only:

Next rnd: *K2tog, ssk; rep from * to end—10 sts rem.

All sizes:

Knit 2 rnds. Break yarn, leaving a 6" (15 cm) tail. Thread tail onto tapestry needle and draw through rem sts, pull closed, and fasten off inside.

Finishing

Weave in ends. Block.

Key

▮ knit with MC

⊞ knit with CC1

▣ knit with CC2

☐ pattern repeat

Mixed Berries

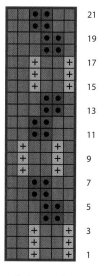

6-st repeat

Tanis SHAWL

In this triangular shawl design, the spine has been reworked and hidden in plain sight. Asymmetrical, it is a piece of the border pattern taken out of context and beaded to emphasize its lovely draping stitches down into the leafy edging.

Finished Measurements
About 59" (150 cm) wingspan and 17" (43 cm) deep.

Yarn
Fingering weight (#1 Super Fine)

Shown here: The Uncommon Thread Heavenly Fingering (70% baby alpaca, 20% silk, 10% cashmere; 440 yd [402 m]/100 g): leaden, 1 hank.

Needles
U.S. size 5 (3.75 mm): 24" (60 cm) circular (cir).

Adjust needle size if necessary to obtain the correct gauge.

Notions
Markers (m); 274 size 6/0 seed beads; size 8 (1.5 mm) steel crochet hook; tapestry needle.

Gauge
21 sts and 31 rows = 4" (10 cm) in St st.

ROMI HILL

NOTE

✪ Markers are used to delineate the lace spine. The markers will be moved several times in the course of knitting the shawl.

Stitch Guide

Place Bead

Slide bead onto crochet hook, insert crochet hook pwise into st and sl st onto crochet hook, slide bead down hook onto st, then return st to left needle and k1.

Shawl

Using the knitted cast-on method (see Techniques), CO 7 sts. Do not join.

Work Rows 1–8 of Chart A, placing markers as indicated on Row 1—31 sts.

Work Rows 1–8 of Chart B nine times, removing existing markers and placing new markers as indicated on Row 1, and working patt reps outlined in red as many times as indicated (i.e. work each patt rep 1 time the first time you work Chart B, then work first patt rep 2 times and second patt rep 3 times the second time through Chart B, etc.)—247 sts.

Work Rows 1–6 of Chart C, removing existing markers and placing new markers as indicated on Row 1, and working each patt rep outlined in red 8 times—293 sts.

Work Rows 1–16 of Chart D 2 times, removing existing markers and placing new markers as indicated on Row 1, and working patt rep outlined in red as many times as indicated (i.e., on first time through work patt rep 17 times, on second time through work patt rep 19 times)—357 sts.

Edging

Row 1: (RS) [K1, yo, k1] into same st, purl to last st, [k1, yo, k1] into same st—361 sts.

Row 2: K3 tbl, p25, p1f&b (see Techniques), [p15, p1f&b] 19 times, p25, k3 tbl—381 sts.

Row 3: K3 tbl, purl to last 3 sts, k3 tbl.

BO as foll: *Use the knitted method to CO 2 sts, k2tog tbl, place bead on next st but do not knit it (leave st on left needle), knit beaded st tbl, pass first st on right needle over second to BO 1 st, BO 3 sts, sl 1 st from right needle to left needle; rep from * until 1 st rem, CO 2 sts, k2tog tbl, place bead on next st but do not knit it, knit beaded st tbl, pass first st on right needle over second to BO 1 st.

Finishing

Weave in ends. Wet block, pinning out each point of edging.

Key

☐	k on RS; p on WS
·	p on RS; k on WS
⅄	k1 tbl on RS
⅄	k1 tbl on WS
○	yo
╱	k2tog
╲	ssk
⟋	k3tog
⟍	k3tog tbl
▢	pattern repeat
❘	marker position
▪	place bead (see Stitch Guide)
⌣	[k1, yo, k1] in same st

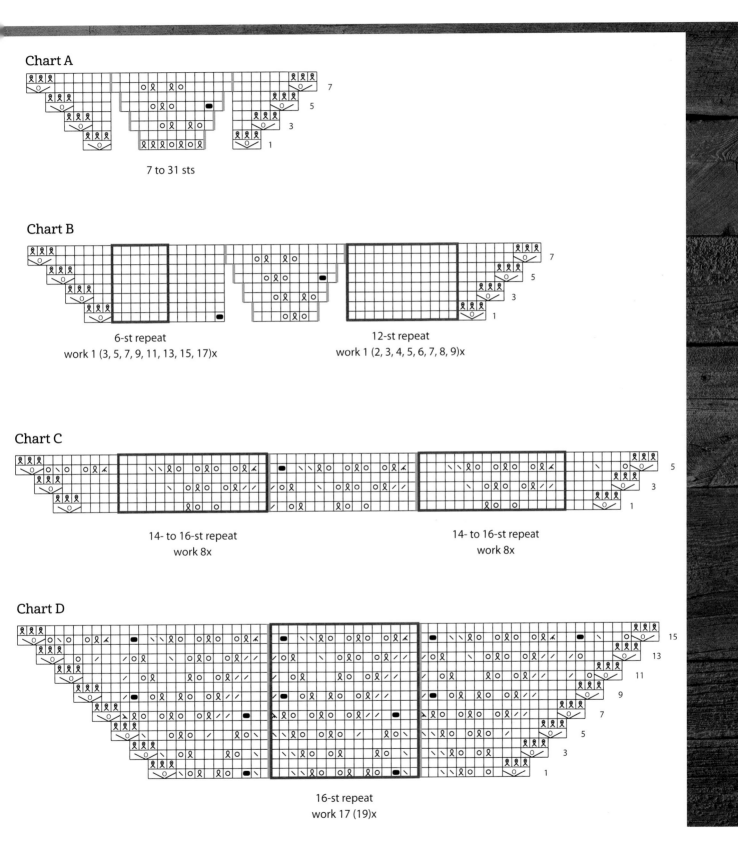

Chart A

7 to 31 sts

Chart B

6-st repeat
work 1 (3, 5, 7, 9, 11, 13, 15, 17)x

12-st repeat
work 1 (2, 3, 4, 5, 6, 7, 8, 9)x

Chart C

14- to 16-st repeat
work 8x

14- to 16-st repeat
work 8x

Chart D

16-st repeat
work 17 (19)x

Momentum MITTENS

Let the yarn do the work in these wardrobe staple mittens! Self-striping yarn creates chunky stripes in bright shades, while the simple twisted cables climb up the hand vertically. The staggering of the cables reflects the natural shape of the hand while the cables around the cuff help the mitts stay snug against the wrist, blocking any drafts.

Finished Size
About 6¾" (17 cm) circumference.

Yarn
Sport weight (#2 Fine)

Shown here: String Theory Colorworks Momentum (100% superwash merino; 274 yd [251 m]/100 g): gamma ray, 1 hank.

Needles
U.S. size 3 (3.25 mm): set of 4 double-pointed (dpn).

Adjust needle size if necessary to obtain the correct gauge.

Notions
Markers (m); cable needle (cn); tapestry needle; waste yarn.

Gauge
22½ sts and 30 rows = 4" (10 cm) in rev St st.

TANIS GRAY

Right Mitten

CUFF

CO 44 sts, place marker (pm) and join to work in the round, taking care not to twist sts.

Begin cabled rib:

Rnd 1: *K2, p2; rep from * to end.

Rnd 2: *1/1 LC (see Stitch Guide), p2; rep from * to end.

Rep Rnds 1–2 thirteen more times.

Next rnd: P4, pm, work patt as established over 14 sts, pm, purl to end.

Cont in patt, keeping 14 sts between m in cabled rib and all other sts in rev St st, for 4 more rnds.

THUMB GUSSET

Rnd 1: Work 22 sts in patt, pm for gusset, M1P (see Techniques), p1, M1P, pm for gusset, purl to end—46 sts; 3 sts between gusset m.

Rnd 2: Work in patt to gusset m, sl m, purl to m, sl m, purl to end.

Rnd 3: Work in patt to gusset m, sl m, M1P, purl to m, M1P, sl m, purl to end—2 sts inc'd.

Rep Rnds 2–3 five more times, then Rnd 2 once—58 sts; 15 sts between gusset m.

Next rnd: Work in patt to gusset m, remove m, place 15 sts on waste yarn for thumb, CO 1 st, remove m, purl to end—44 sts.

HAND

Cont in patt until mitten measures 8¼" (21 cm) from CO.

Next rnd: P4, remove m, p4, pm, work patt as established over 6 sts, pm, p4, remove m, purl to end.

Cont in patt, keeping 6 sts between m in cabled rib and all other sts in rev St st, until mitten measures 9" (23 cm), ending with Rnd 2 of cabled rib.

Purl 3 rnds, removing m.

Shape top:

Rnd 1: P22, pm, purl to end.

Rnd 2: [Ssk, purl to 2 sts before m, k2tog], sl m 2 times—4 sts dec'd.

Rep Rnd 2 eight more times—8 sts rem.

Break yarn leaving a 10" (25.5 cm) tail for grafting. Turn mitten inside out, place first 4 sts on one dpn and rem 4 sts on a second dpn, and use Kitchener st (see Techniques) to graft top closed.

THUMB

Place 15 held sts on dpn. Join yarn. Pick up and knit 1 st where thumb joins hand, p15 , pm for beg of rnd—16 sts.

Work even in rev St st until thumb measures 1¾" (4.5 cm) from join.

Next rnd: *P2tog; rep from * to end—8 sts rem.

Rep last rnd—4 sts rem.

Break yarn, leaving a 6" (15 cm) tail. Thread tail onto tapestry needle and draw through rem sts, pull closed, and fasten off inside.

Left Mitten

CUFF

CO 44 sts, place marker (pm) and join to work in the round, taking care not to twist sts.

Begin cabled rib:

Rnd 1: *P2, k2; rep from * to end.

Rnd 2: *P2, 1/1 LC; rep from * to end.

Rep Rnds 1–2 thirteen more times.

Next rnd: P26, pm, work patt as established over 14 sts, pm, purl to end.

Cont in patt, keeping 14 sts between m in cabled rib and all other sts in rev St st, for 4 more rnds.

THUMB GUSSET

Rnd 1: P21, pm for gusset, M1P, p1, M1P, pm for gusset, work in patt to end—46 sts; 3 sts between gusset m.

Rnd 2: Purl to gusset m, sl m, purl to m, sl m, work in patt to end.

Rnd 3: Purl to gusset m, sl m, M1P, purl to m, M1P, sl m, work in patt to end—2 sts inc'd.

Rep Rnds 2–3 five more times, then Rnd 2 once—58 sts; 15 sts between gusset m.

Next rnd: Purl to gusset m, remove m, place 15 sts on waste yarn for thumb, CO 1 st, remove m, work in patt to end—44 sts.

HAND

Cont in patt until mitten measures 8¼" (21 cm) from CO.

Next rnd: P26, remove m, p4, pm, work patt as established over 6 sts, pm, p4, remove m, purl to end.

Cont in patt, keeping 6 sts between m in cabled rib and all other sts in rev St st, until mitten measures 9" (23 cm), ending with Rnd 2 of cabled rib.

Purl 3 rnds, removing m.

Shape top as for Right Mitten.

THUMB

Work as for Right Mitten.

Finishing

Weave in ends. Block.

Little Vine BERET

This design celebrates how a few simple stitches—knits and purls, increases and decreases—can create familiar patterns, like those found in nature. For this hat, a simple vine pattern starts after the ribbed brim and flows through the body, neatly into the decreases.

Finished Size
20" (51 cm) brim circumference

Yarn
Aran weight (#4 Medium)

Shown here: Quince and Co. Osprey (100% American wool; 170 yd [155 m]/100g): snap pea, 1 hank.

Needles
Ribbing: U.S. size 7 (4.5 mm): 16" circular (cir).

Body: U.S. size 8 (5 mm): 16" cir and set of 4 double-pointed (dpn).

Adjust needle size if necessary to obtain the correct gauge.

Notions
Marker (m); tapestry needle.

Gauge
16 sts and 22 rows = 4" (10 cm) in Little Vine chart on larger needles.

MELISSA LABARRE

Beret

With smaller cir needle, CO 80 sts. Place marker (pm) and join for working in the round, being careful not to twist sts. Work in k1, p1 rib for 1" (2.5 cm).

Inc rnd: *K1, k1f&b; rep from * to end—120 sts.

Change to larger needle. Purl 1 rnd. Work Rnds 1–12 of Little Vine chart once, then Rnds 1–6 once. Hat measures about 4¾" (12 cm) from CO.

Crown

Note: Change to dpns when there are too few sts to work comfortably on cir needle.

Work Rnds 1–21 of Crown chart—10 sts rem.

Break yarn, leaving a 6" (15 cm) tail. Thread tail onto tapestry needle and draw through rem sts, pull closed, and fasten off inside.

Finishing

Weave in ends. Block over a 10" (25.5 cm) dinner plate.

Key

☐	k
·	p
○	yo
╱	k2tog
╲	ssk
☐	pattern repeat

Little Vine

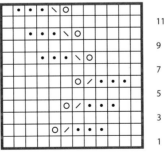

12 st repeat

Crown

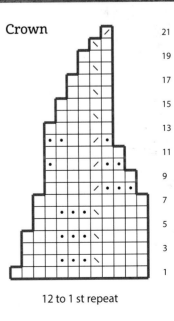

12 to 1 st repeat

Leeside SHAWL

This shawl is slightly asymmetrical in shape and design but very simple to knit. It is cast on at one wing tip with a few stitches and simply knit into a widening triangle. The tiny lace border then turns the corner and becomes a sideways bind off. This shawl is simple to enlarge if you have extra yarn by repeating the last chart as many times as desired.

Finished Size
About 44" (112 cm) wingspan and 21" (53.5 cm) deep.

Yarn
Fingering weight (#1 Super Fine)

Shown here: Hazel Knits Artisan Sock (90% superwash merino, 10% nylon; 400 yd [366 m]/120 g): beachglass, 1 hank.

Needles
U.S. size 5 (3.75 mm): 24" (60 cm) circular (cir).

Notions
Marker (m) (optional); tapestry needle.

Gauge
20 sts and 28 rows = 4" (10 cm) in St st.

JUDY MARPLES

NOTES

✪ Shawl is cast on at one wing tip and worked across to the other wing tip in a gradually widening triangle. A circular needle is used to accommodate the growing number of sts.

✪ The narrow lace edging is worked along the straight edge of the triangle simultaneously with the body. When the body is complete, the edging is continued around the corner and along the adjacent side to the opposite wing tip.

✪ A placement line for an optional marker dividing the edging from the body of the shawl is shown on the charts.

Shawl

BODY

CO 4 sts. Do not join. Knit 2 rows.

Work Rows 1–36 of Chart A—22 sts.

Work Rows 1–48 of Chart B—46 sts.

Work Rows 1–24 of Chart C seven

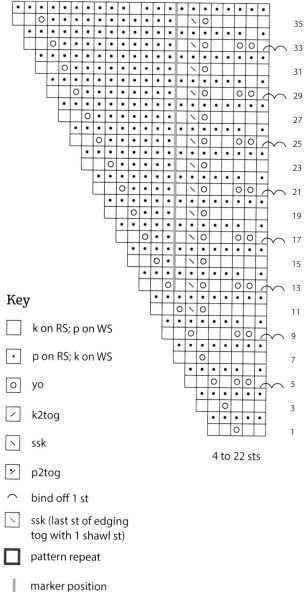

Chart A

4 to 22 sts

Key

☐	k on RS; p on WS
•	p on RS; k on WS
○	yo
╱	k2tog
╲	ssk
⟋	p2tog
⌒	bind off 1 st
╲	ssk (last st of edging tog with 1 shawl st)
▢	pattern repeat
▏	marker position

times, working 3 additional 4-st patt reps every 24 rows—130 sts.

EDGING

Next row: (RS) Work Row 1 of Chart D over 9 sts (8 edging sts plus 1 st from body of shawl), turn—129 sts rem.

Next row: (WS) Work Row 2 of chart.

Cont as established, work Rows 3-12 of chart once, then Rows 13-16 fifty-nine times, then Rows 13-14 once—8 sts rem.

BO all sts.

Finishing

Weave in ends but do not trim. Wet block, pinning out the points of the edging. Trim ends after shawl is dry.

Chart B

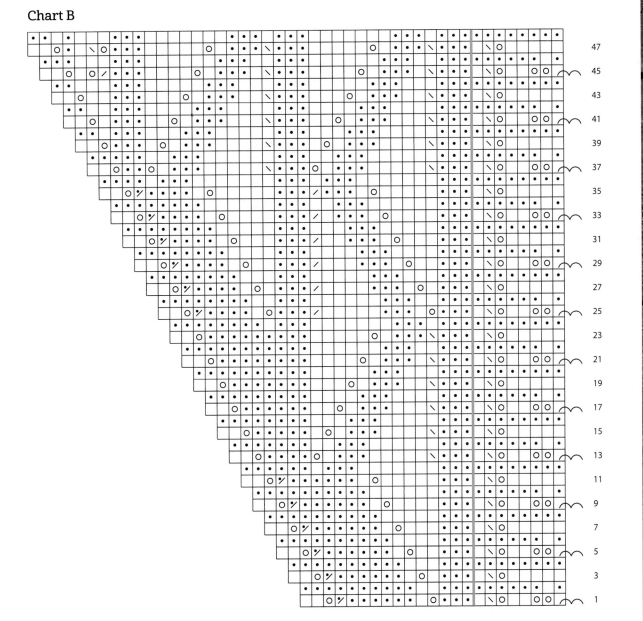

22 to 46 sts

Chart C

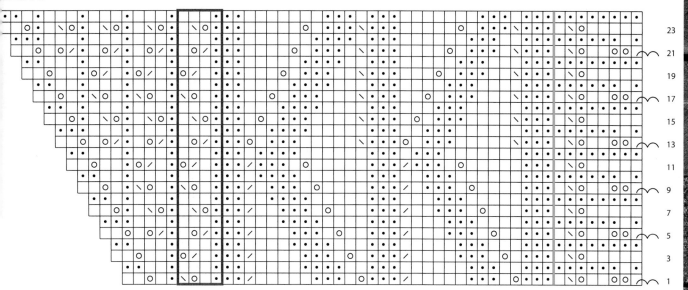

4 st repeat

Key

☐	k on RS; p on WS
•	p on RS; k on WS
O	yo
/	k2tog
\	ssk
⅄	p2tog
⌢	bind off 1 st
\	ssk (last st of edging tog with 1 shawl st)
▣	pattern repeat
❘	marker position

Chart D

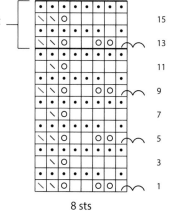

4 row repeat

8 sts

Spraying Waves COWL

Is there anything easier than a cowl? Cast on your stitches, join in the round, and off you go! This cowl may look hard but is actually quite easy to do. Most of the rounds are either knitted or purled with one row of more complex stitching. Two bright contrasting colors were used, but get creative and use two similar toned colors or even the same color! The waves will add wonderful texture.

Finished Size
25½" (65 cm) circumference and 12" (30.5 cm) tall.

Yarn
DK weight (#3 Light)

Shown here: Berroco Weekend DK (75% acrylic, 25% Peruvian cotton; 268 yd [247 m]/100 g): #2956 Swimming Hole (blue) (MC), 1 hank #2925 Taffy (lt green) (CC), 1 hank.

Needles
U.S. size 6 (4 mm): 16" (40 cm) circular (cir).

Adjust needle size if necessary to obtain the correct gauge.

Notions
Marker (m); cable needle (cn); tapestry needle.

Gauge
22 sts and 36 rnds = 4" (10 cm) in Waves st.

MARGAUX HUFNAGEL

NOTES

✪ Cowl is worked in the round.

✪ Take care to carry the yarn loosely behind the slipped stitches.

✪ Do not cut yarns at color changes. Carry old yarn loosely up wrong side of work until it is needed again.

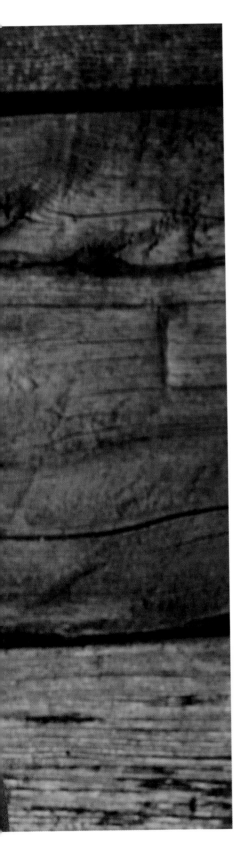

1/1 RC

Sl 1 st onto cn, hold to back, k1, k1 from cn.

1/1 LC

Sl 1 st onto cn, hold to front, k1, k1 from cn.

Waves Stitch:
(multiple of 10 sts)

Rnds 1–3: With MC, knit.

Rnd 4: With CC, knit.

Rnd 5: With CC, *p3, k3, p4; rep from * to end.

Rnds 6–9: With MC, *k3, sl 3 pwise with yarn in back (wyb), k4; rep from * to end.

Rnd 10: With MC, *k2, 1/1 RC, sl 1 pwise wyb, 1/1 LC, k3; rep from * to end.

Rnds 11–13: With MC, knit.

Rnd 14: With CC, knit.

Rnd 15: With CC, *k1, p7, k2; rep from * to end.

Rnds 16–19: With MC, *sl 1 pwise wyb, k7, sl 2 pwise wyb; rep from * to end.

Rnd 20: With MC, *1/1 LC, k5, 1/1 RC, sl 1 pwise wyb; rep from * to end.

Rep Rnds 1–20 for patt.

Cowl

With CC, CO 140 sts. Place marker (pm) and join for working in the round, being careful not to twist sts. Purl 1 rnd. Work Rnds 1–20 of Waves st 5 times. With MC, knit 3 rnds. With CC, knit 1 rnd. BO all sts pwise with CC.

Finishing

Weave in ends. Block.

A Case of Lace SOCKS

Inspiration for these socks was found in the Joni Mitchell song "A Case of You." We all know that a knitter will add a little love in each and every stitch, and Joni's song tells us something similar. The construction is toe-up, with the design already starting in the toe section.

Finished Size
About 7½ (7¾, 8)" (19 [19.5, 20.5] cm) foot circumference and 9 (9¼, 9½)" (23 [23.5, 24.5] cm) foot length (adjustable).

Socks shown measure 7½" (19 cm).

Yarn
Fingering weight (#1 Super Fine)

Shown here: Wollmeise Twin Sockenwolle (80% merino wool, 20% nylon; 510 yd [466 m]/150 g): olio vergine, 1 hank.

Needles
U.S. size 1½ (2.5 mm) set of 4 double-pointed (dpn).

Adjust needle size if necessary to obtain the correct gauge.

Notions
Markers (m); tapestry needle; cable needle (cn).

Gauge
28 sts and 42 rnds = 4" (10 cm) in St st.

MARJAN HAMMINK

NOTES

✪ These socks are worked from the toe up with a heel flap and gusset.

✪ When right and left sides of the sock are mentioned, they refer to left and right as worn.

✪ Socks are worked as mirror images by twisting some of the cables to the right on the first sock and to the left on the second sock (see charts and key).

Key

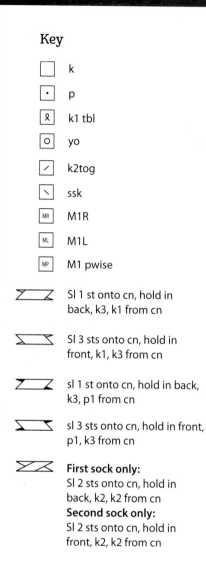

☐   k

•   p

Ɋ   k1 tbl

○   yo

╱   k2tog

╲   ssk

MR   M1R

ML   M1L

MP   M1 pwise

Sl 1 st onto cn, hold in back, k3, k1 from cn

Sl 3 sts onto cn, hold in front, k1, k3 from cn

sl 1 st onto cn, hold in back, k3, p1 from cn

sl 3 sts onto cn, hold in front, p1, k3 from cn

First sock only:
Sl 2 sts onto cn, hold in back, k2, k2 from cn
Second sock only:
Sl 2 sts onto cn, hold in front, k2, k2 from cn

Top of Toe

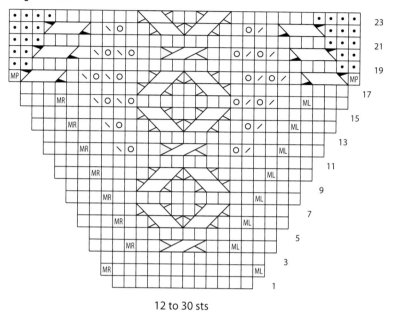

12 to 30 sts

Bottom of Toe size 7½" (19 cm)

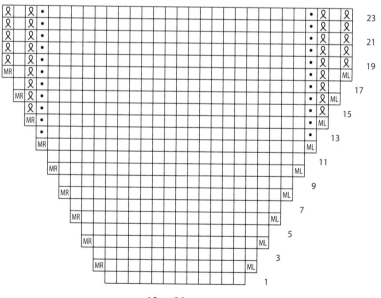

12 to 30 sts

Bottom of Toe size 7¾" (19.5 cm)

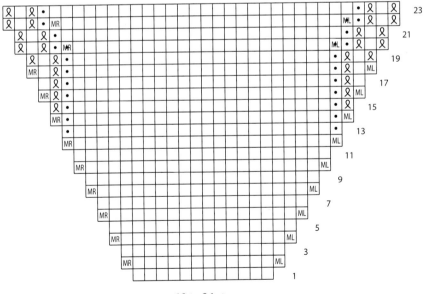

12 to 32 sts

Bottom of Toe size 8" (20.5 cm)

12 to 34 sts

Toe

Using Judy's Magic Cast-On (see Techniques), CO 24 sts divided over 2 needles—12 sts each needle. Place marker (pm) and join to work in the round.

Rnd 1: Work Rnd 1 of Top of Toe chart over first needle, work Rnd 1 of Bottom of Toe chart for your size over second needle.

Cont in patt through Rnd 23 of charts—60 (62, 64) sts; 30 sts for instep and 30 (32, 34) sts for sole.

Foot

Rnd 1: Work Rnd 1 of Instep chart over first 30 sts, pm, k1 tbl, k1, k1 tbl, p1, k22 (k24, 26), p1, k1 tbl, k1, k1 tbl.

Cont in patt, work Rnds 2–6 of Instep chart once, then rep Rnds 7–30 until sock measures 5" (12.5 cm), or desired length.

Key

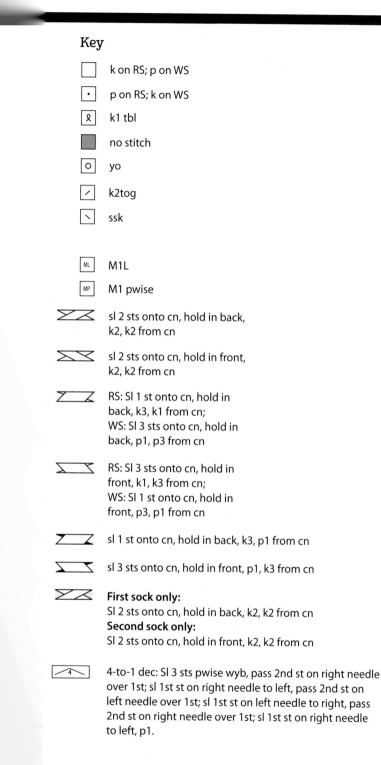

☐	k on RS; p on WS
☐•	p on RS; k on WS
☒	k1 tbl
▨	no stitch
☐○	yo
⟋	k2tog
⟍	ssk
ML	M1L
MP	M1 pwise

⟍⟋ sl 2 sts onto cn, hold in back, k2, k2 from cn

⟋⟍ sl 2 sts onto cn, hold in front, k2, k2 from cn

⟋⟍ RS: Sl 1 st onto cn, hold in back, k3, k1 from cn;
WS: Sl 3 sts onto cn, hold in back, p1, p3 from cn

⟍⟋ RS: Sl 3 sts onto cn, hold in front, k1, k3 from cn;
WS: Sl 1 st onto cn, hold in front, p3, p1 from cn

⟋⟍ sl 1 st onto cn, hold in back, k3, p1 from cn

⟍⟋ sl 3 sts onto cn, hold in front, p1, k3 from cn

⟍⟋ **First sock only:**
Sl 2 sts onto cn, hold in back, k2, k2 from cn
Second sock only:
Sl 2 sts onto cn, hold in front, k2, k2 from cn

⟋4⟍ 4-to-1 dec: Sl 3 sts pwise wyb, pass 2nd st on right needle over 1st; sl 1st st on right needle to left, pass 2nd st on left needle over 1st; sl 1st st on left needle to right, pass 2nd st on right needle over 1st; sl 1st st on right needle to left, p1.

Left Gusset

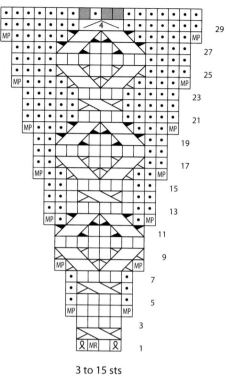

3 to 15 sts

Right Gusset

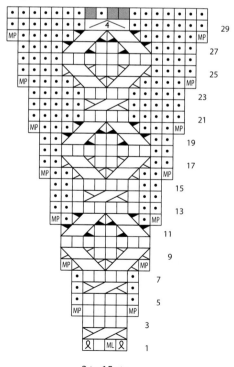

3 to 15 sts

Gussets

Rnd 1: Work in patt to last 3 sts, pm for new beg of rnd.

Rnd 2: Work Rnd 1 of Left Gusset chart over 3 sts, sl m, work 30 instep sts in patt, sl m, work Rnd 1 of Right Gusset chart over 3 sts, pm, work in patt to end—62 (64, 66) sts.

Cont in patt through Rnd 29 of Gusset charts—84 (86, 88) sts.

Turn Heel

Short-row 1: (RS) Work Rnd 30 of Left Gusset chart, sl m, work 30 instep sts in patt, sl m, work Rnd 30 of Right Gusset chart, sl m, p1, k21 (23, 25), wrap next st, turn.

Short-row 2: (WS) P20 (22, 24), wrap next st, turn.

Short-row 3: Knit to 1 st before previous wrapped st, wrap next st, turn.

Short-row 4: Purl to 1 st before previous wrapped st, wrap next st, turn.

Rep Short-rows 3 and 4 three (four, five) more times—12 sts rem unwrapped in center of heel.

Next row: (RS) K12, [pick up and knit wrap tog with wrapped st] 5 (6, 7) times, p1, remove m, p15, sl m, work 30 instep sts in patt, sl m, p15, remove m, p1, [pick up and knit wrap tog with wrapped st tbl] 5 (6, 7) times. Do not turn.

Redistribute sts as foll: 30 instep sts on hold on one needle, rem 54 (56, 58) gusset and sole sts on two other needles.

Heel Flap

Row 1: (RS) K16 (17, 18), ssk, turn—1 st dec'd.

Row 2: (WS) Sl 1 pwise with yarn in front (wyf), p20 (22, 24), p2tog, turn—1 st dec'd.

Row 3: Sl 1 pwise with yarn in back (wyb), k5 (6, 7), pm, work Heel Flap chart over 10 sts, pm, k5 (6, 7), ssk, turn—1 st dec'd.

Row 4: Sl 1 pwise with yarn in front (wyf), p5 (6, 7), sl m, work Heel Flap chart, sl m, p5 (6, 7), p2tog, turn—1 st dec'd.

Rep Rows 3–4 nine more times, working Rows 1–4 of Heel Flap chart once, then repeating Rows 5–12—32 (34, 36) sole sts rem.

Resume working in the round:

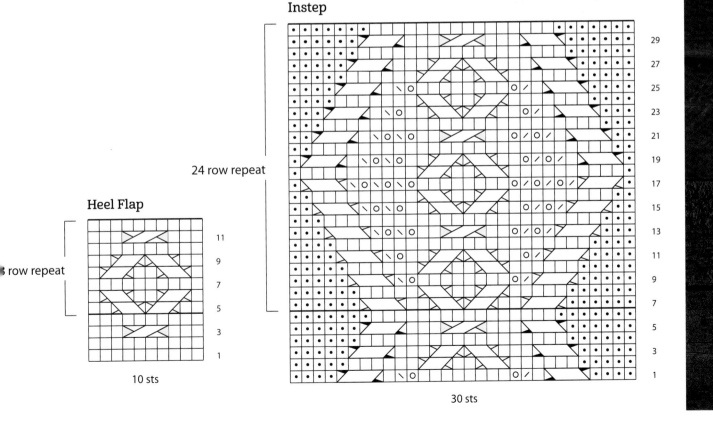

Instep

24 row repeat

Heel Flap

row repeat

10 sts

30 sts

Key

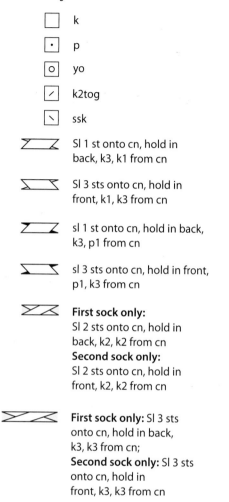

- ☐ k
- · p
- ⊙ yo
- ╱ k2tog
- ╲ ssk

Sl 1 st onto cn, hold in back, k3, k1 from cn

Sl 3 sts onto cn, hold in front, k1, k3 from cn

sl 1 st onto cn, hold in back, k3, p1 from cn

sl 3 sts onto cn, hold in front, p1, k3 from cn

First sock only:
Sl 2 sts onto cn, hold in back, k2, k2 from cn
Second sock only:
Sl 2 sts onto cn, hold in front, k2, k2 from cn

First sock only: Sl 3 sts onto cn, hold in back, k3, k3 from cn;
Second sock only: Sl 3 sts onto cn, hold in front, k3, k3 from cn

Front of Leg

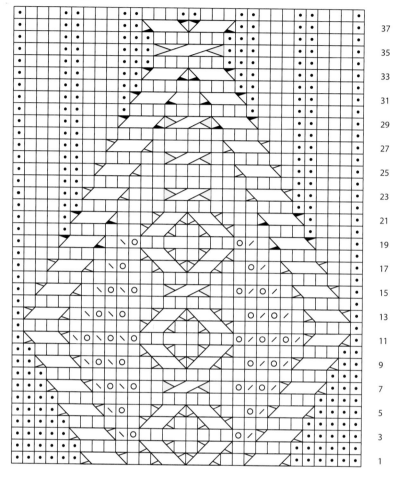

30 sts

Key

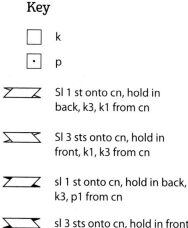

☐	k
⊡	p
⧄	Sl 1 st onto cn, hold in back, k3, k1 from cn
⧄	Sl 3 sts onto cn, hold in front, k1, k3 from cn
⧄	sl 1 st onto cn, hold in back, k3, p1 from cn
⧄	sl 3 sts onto cn, hold in front, p1, k3 from cn

Back of Leg size 7¾" (19.5 cm)

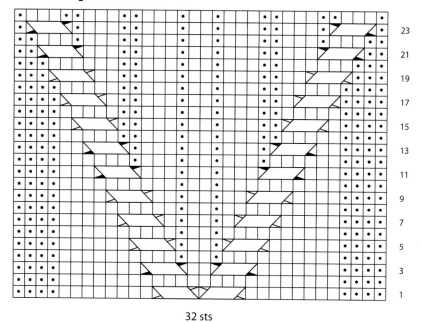

23
21
19
17
15
13
11
9
7
5
3
1

32 sts

Back of Leg size 8" (20.5 cm)

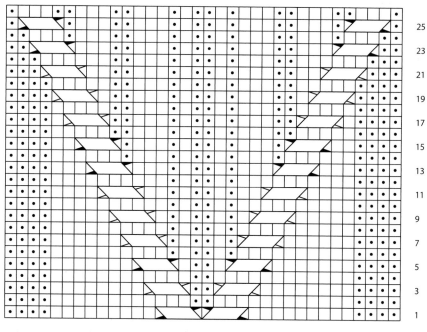

25
23
21
19
17
15
13
11
9
7
5
3
1

34 sts

Next rnd: Sl 1 pwise wyb, k5 (6, 7), sl m, work Heel Flap chart, sl m, k5 (6, 7), ssk, p4, pm, work 30 instep sts in patt, pm, p4, k2tog, k5 (6, 7), sl m, work Heel Flap chart, sl m, k6 (7, 8), p4—60 (62, 64) sts rem; 30 sts for instep/front of leg and 30 (32, 34) sts for back of leg.

Leg

Note: The beginning of the Front Leg chart will not necessarily line up with the beginning of the Back Leg chart. After establishing the Front Leg chart, you will begin working the Back Leg chart at the next opportunity while maintaining the continuity of the cable pattern.

Rnd 1: Sl m, work 30 instep sts in patt, sl m, p4, knit to m, work 10 heel flap sts in patt, sl m, k6 (7, 8), p4.

Cont in patt for desired length, ending with Rnd 30 of Instep chart. Switch to working Front of Leg chart over these 30 sts.

At about the same time, after completing Rnd 12 of Heel Flap chart, remove m around 10 heel flap sts and begin working Back of Leg chart for your size over 30 (32, 34) back leg sts.

After completing chart(s), work in ribbing as established by last rnd of chart. When both Front of Leg and Back of Leg charts are complete, work an additional 10 (12, 14) rnds in rib to complete cuff.

BO all sts using Jeny's Surprisingly Stretchy Bind-Off (see Techniques).

Finishing

Weave in ends. Block lightly.

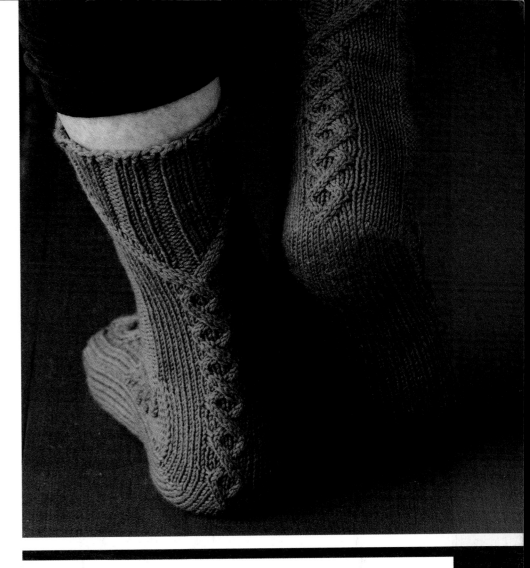

Back of Leg size 7½" (19 cm)

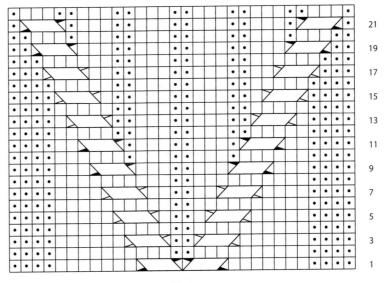

30 sts

Laure MITTENS

Hand-dyed yarns are lovely, but not every knitter is keen on the way the colors can pool. For these mittens, a slipped-stitch pattern shuffles colors around and reduces the tendency of hand-dyes to stripe. Because the silk/alpaca blend trades elasticity for its luscious softness, the yarn is knit at a tighter-than-typical gauge that will keep hands toasty warm.

Finished Size
6½ (8, 8¾)" (16.5 [20.5, 22] cm) in circumference and about 9 (9½, 9¾)" (23 [24, 25] cm) long.

Mittens shown measure 8" (20.5 cm).

Yarn
Worsted weight (#4 Medium)

Shown here: Lorna's Laces Shepherd Worsted (100% superwash wool; 225 yd [206 m]/113 g): Christmas at Downton, 1 hank.

Needles
U.S. size 9 (5.5 mm): set of 4 double-pointed (dpn).

Adjust needle size if necessary to obtain the correct gauge.

Notions
Marker (m); waste yarn; tapestry needle.

Gauge
22 sts and 44 rnds = 4" (10 cm) in garter slipped st.

CAROL J. SULCOSKI

NOTES

✪ Mittens are worked in the round from the cuff up.

✪ Stitches for thumb opening are knit onto waste yarn until mitten hand is finished, then waste yarn is removed and live sts are used for thumb.

Stitch Guide

**Slipped-Stitch Rib
(even number of sts)**

Rnd 1: *Sl 1 pwise with yarn in back (wyb), p1; rep from * to end.

Rnd 2: *K1, p1; rep from * to end.

Rep Rnds 1–2 for patt.

**Garter Slipped Stitch
(even number of sts)**

Rnd 1: Knit.

Rnd 2: Purl.

Rnd 3: *Sl 1 pwise wyb, k1; rep from * to end.

Rnd 4: *Sl 1 pwise wyb, p1; rep from * to end.

Rep Rnds 1–4 for patt.

HAND

Work even in garter slipped stitch patt until mitten measures about 7¾ (8, 8¼)" (19.5 [20.5, 21] cm) from CO, ending with Rnd 4 of patt.

Shape top:

Dec rnd: *K4 (5, 6), k2tog; rep from * five more times, k0 (2, 0)—30 (38, 42) sts rem.

Work 3 rnds even.

Dec rnd: *K3 (4, 5), k2tog; rep from * five more times, k0 (2, 0)—24 (32, 36) sts rem.

Work 3 rnds even.

Dec rnd: *K2 (3, 4), k2tog; rep from * five more times, k0 (2, 0)—18 (26, 30) sts rem.

Work 3 rnds even.

Dec rnd: Dec rnd: *K1 (2, 3), k2tog; rep from * five more times, k0 (2, 0)—12 (20, 24) sts rem.

Sizes 8¾" (20.5 [22] cm) only:

Work 3 rnds even.

Dec rnd: *K1 (2), k2tog; rep from * five more times, k2 (0)—14 (18) sts rem.

All sizes:

Break yarn, leaving an 18" (45.5 cm) tail. Divide rem sts over two dpn and graft together using Kitchener st (see Techniques).

THUMB

Remove waste yarn and place resulting 7 (8, 9) sts from top opening on one dpn and 7 (8, 9) sts from bottom of opening on a second dpn. Join yarn. Redistributing sts evenly over 3 dpn as you work, knit sts on first needle, pick up and knit 1 st at corner of opening, knit sts on second needle, pick up and knit 1 st at corner of opening—16 (18, 20) sts.

Work in St st until thumb measures 2 (2¼, 2¾)" (5 [5.5, 7] cm) from pick-up rnd.

Right Mitt

CUFF

CO 36 (44, 48) sts. Place marker (pm) and join to work in the round, taking care not to twist sts.

Knit 1 rnd. Purl 1 rnd. Knit 1 rnd.

Work in slipped-stitch rib until cuff measures 3" (7.5 cm) from CO, ending with Rnd 2 of patt.

Knit 1 rnd. Purl 1 rnd.

Begin working in garter slipped stitch patt. Work even until mitten measures about 5½ (5¾, 6)" (14 [14.5, 15] cm) from CO, ending with Rnd 4 of patt.

THUMB OPENING

Next rnd: With waste yarn, k7 (8, 9), then slip these 7 (8, 9) sts back to left needle. Cut waste yarn. With main yarn, work garter slipped st patt to end of rnd.

Dec rnd: *[K2tog] 4 (4, 5) times, k0 (1, 0); rep from * once more—8 (10, 10) sts rem.

Dec rnd: *[K2tog] 2 times, k0 (1, 1); rep from * once more—4 (5, 5) sts rem.

Break yarn, leaving a 6" (15 cm) tail. Thread tail onto tapestry needle and draw through rem sts, pull snug to tighten, and fasten off inside.

Left Mitten

CUFF

Work as for Right Mitten.

THUMB OPENING

Next rnd: Work 11 (14, 15) sts in patt. Drop main yarn. With waste yarn, k7 (8, 9), then slip these 7 (8, 9) sts back to left needle. Cut waste yarn. With main yarn, work garter slipped st patt to end of rnd.

HAND

Work as for Right Mitten.

THUMB

Work as for Right Mitten.

Finishing

Weave in ends. Block gently.

Abbreviations

beg(s)	begin(s); beginning		**pm**	place marker
BO	bind off		**psso**	pass slipped stitch over
cir	circular		**pwise**	purlwise; as if to purl
cm	centimeter(s)		**rem**	remain(s); remaining
cn	cable needle		**rep**	repeat(s); repeating
CO	cast on		**rev St st**	reverse stockinette stitch
cont	continue(s); continuing		**rnd(s)**	round(s)
dec(s)('d)	decrease(s); decreasing; decreased		**RS**	right side
dpn	double-pointed needles		**sl**	slip
foll(s)	follow(s); following		**sl st**	slip st (slip stitch purl-wise unless otherwise indicated)
g	gram(s)		**ssk**	slip, slip, knit (decrease)
inc(s)('d)	increase(s); increasing; increase(d)		**st(s)**	stitch(es)
k	knit		**St st**	stockinette stitch
k1f&b	knit into the front and back of same stitch		**tbl**	through back loop
k2tog	knit 2 stitches together		**tog**	together
k3tog	knit 3 stitches together		**WS**	wrong side
kwise	knitwise, as if to knit		**wyb**	with yarn in back
m	marker(s)		**wyf**	with yarn in front
mm	millimeter(s)		**yd**	yard(s)
M1	make one (increase)		**yo**	yarnover
oz	ounce		*	repeat starting point
p	purl		**	repeat starting point
p1f&b	purl into front and back of same stitch		()	alternate measurements and/or instructions
p2tog	purl 2 stitches together		[]	work instructions as a group a specified number of times
patt(s)	pattern(s)			

Techniques

Cast-Ons

BACKWARD-LOOP CAST-ON

*Loop working yarn and place it on needle backward so that it doesn't unwind. Repeat from *.

CABLE CAST-ON

If there are no stitches on the needle, make a slipknot of working yarn and place it on the needle, then use the knitted method to cast on one more stitch—two stitches on needle. Hold needle with working yarn in your left hand with the wrong side of the work facing you. *Insert right needle between the first two stitches on left needle **(Fig. 1)**, wrap yarn around needle as if to knit, draw yarn through **(Fig. 2)**, and place new loop on left needle **(Fig. 3)** to form a new stitch. Repeat from * for the desired number of stitches, always working between the first two stitches on the left needle.

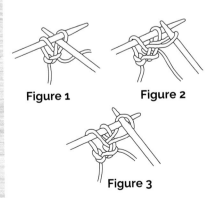

Figure 1   Figure 2

Figure 3

CROCHET CHAIN PROVISIONAL CAST-ON

With waste yarn and crochet hook, make a loose crochet chain (see page 139) about four stitches more than you need to cast on. With knitting needle, working yarn, and beginning two stitches from end of chain, pick up and knit one stitch through the back loop of each crochet chain **(Fig. 1)** for desired number of stitches. When you're ready to work in the opposite direction, pull out the crochet chain to expose live stitches **(Fig. 2)**.

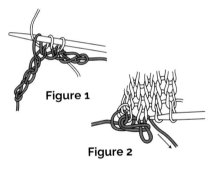

Figure 1

Figure 2

INVISIBLE PROVISIONAL CAST-ON

Make a loose slipknot of working yarn and place it on the right needle. Hold a length of contrasting waste yarn next to the slipknot and around your left thumb; hold working yarnover your left index finger. *Bring the right needle forward under waste yarn, over working yarn, grab a loop of working yarn **(Fig. 1)**, then bring the needle back behind the working yarn and grab a second loop **(Fig. 2)**.

Repeat from * for the desired number of stitches. When you're ready to work in the opposite direction, place the exposed loops on a knitting needle as you pull out the waste yarn.

Figure 1

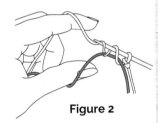

Figure 2

KNITTED CAST-ON

Make a slipknot of working yarn and place it on the left needle if there are no stitches already there. *Use the right needle to knit the first stitch (or slipknot) on left needle **(Fig. 1)** and place new loop onto left needle to form a new stitch **(Fig. 2)**. Repeat from * for the desired number of stitches, always working into the last stitch made.

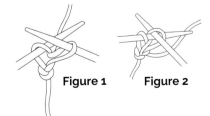

Figure 1   Figure 2

JUDY'S MAGIC CAST-ON

This amazingly simple cast-on is named for its founder, Judy Becker. It wraps the yarn around two parallel needles in such a way as to mimic a row of stockinette stitch between the two needles.

Leaving a 10" (25.5 cm) tail, drape the yarn over one needle, then hold a second needle parallel to and below the first and on top of the yarn tail **(Fig. 1)**.

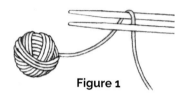

Figure 1

Bring the tail to the back and the ball yarn to the front, then place the thumb and index finger of your left hand between the two strands so that the tail is over your index finger and the ball yarn is over your thumb **(Fig. 2)**. This forms the first stitch on the top needle.

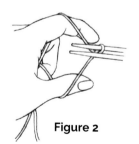

Figure 2

*Continue to hold the two needles parallel and loop the finger yarn over the lower needle by bringing the lower needle over the top of the finger yarn **(Fig. 3)**, then bringing the finger yarn up from below the lower needle, over the top of this needle, then to the back between the two needles.Point the needles downward, bring the bottom needle past the thumb yarn, then bring the thumb yarn to the front between the two needles and over the top needle **(Fig. 4)**.

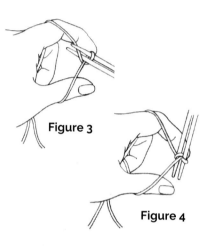

Figure 3

Figure 4

Repeat from * until you have the desired number of stitches on each needle **(Fig. 5)**. Remove both yarn ends from your left hand, rotate the needles like the hands of a clock so that the bottom needle is now on top and both strands of yarn are at the needle tip **(Fig. 6)**.

Figure 5

Figure 6

MOEBIUS CAST-ON

by Cat Bordhi, *Knitscene Accessories* (Interweave, 2012)

A Moebius requires a long circular needle; do not attempt it with one shorter than recommended. A 40" (101.5 cm) length is ideal for hats and a 47" (119.5 cm) length is better for greater circumferences.

Home Position

1. Make a slip knot and slide it to the middle of the cable **(Fig. 1)**.

2. Pick up left needle with right hand and coil it around to form a ring, with the needle pointing up toward the left (you can ignore the right needle).

3. Create a pivot point: with right hand, pinch needle, slip knot, and cable so they can pivot from this one point (yellow star).

4. With left hand, tension yarn and pinch cable (orange star) about 4" (10 cm) away from pivot point. Use left index finger to hold yarn up high (green star). The three stars form a triangle of dotted lines: the cable is the base, the yarn is the right side, and your left hand is the left side.

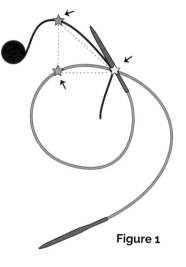

Figure 1

Start the Moebius Cast-On (MCO)

1. The needle points at you, dives under the cable, stands up in the middle of the triangle, presses down on the yarn and swings back under the cable to you, bringing along the yarn (the first stitch). The needle swings from home position and back to home position like a child on a swing. **(Fig. 2)**

2. Next, the needle swoops up over the yarn (the second stitch, which is just like a yarnover) and is once again in home position.

3. Repeat Steps 1 and 2 until you have the desired number of stitches. Count only the stitches on the needle. Each repeat of Steps 1 and 2 creates two stitches on the needle, which are counted, as well as two stitches on the cable, which are not counted. Do not count the slip knot (it is not on the needle) or those on the cable.

Get Ready to Start Knitting

1. Hold needles crossed together as if about to start knitting, and tug at the cable rings to make them the same size.

2. Spread cast-on stitches until beginning and end are very close.

Figure 2

3. Check for one crossing of needle and cable by going for a "train ride" from the left needle around to the right needle, pressing cables into parallel tracks, pushing twist ahead to determine that there is only one crossing at the end.

4. Place a marker on right needle. Do not skip the marker!

Knit the First Ring

The slip knot, which was on the cable, is now first in line on the left needle. Knit into it and take it off the left needle. Each remaining stitch on the left needle resembles a triangle, with the cable as its base. To knit a triangle, insert the right needle into the front (where the star is), pull a loop of yarn through as usual, then remove the triangle from the left needle. Repeat until all triangles have been knitted and the marker appears beneath the needles on the cable. You have completed the first of two rings. **(Fig. 3)**

The MCO looks like this: All stitches on the needle wrap in same direction. Stitches on cable alternate direction of wrap. Pivot point: Right hand pinches needle, slip knot, and cable.

Figure 3

Remember: Two rings of knitting = 1 Moebius round.

The triangles are now gone, and the stitches on the left needle look more familiar; in fact, they look like they were purled. Continue knitting. If the first stitch appears odd, pull the tail down toward yourself and the stitch will then behave. When the marker appears between the needles (not beneath, as before), this signals the completion of one full round (two rings). Only when the marker appears between the needles (where it could fall off) is a round complete **(Fig. 4)**.

When the marker appears on the cable below the needles, only the first of the two rings that make up a round is done. As you keep knitting, you'll discover that the fabric grows between the cables, pushing them apart.

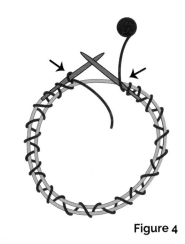

Figure 4

Bind-Offs

SEWN BIND-OFF

This method, worked using a tapestry needle, forms an elastic edge that has a ropy appearance much like a purl row. It is ideal for finishing off garter stitch.

Cut the yarn, leaving a tail about three times the width of the knitting to be bound off, and thread the tail onto a tapestry needle.

Working from right to left, *insert the tapestry needle purlwise (from right to left) through the first two stitches on the left needle tip **(Fig. 1)** and pull the yarn through. Bring tapestry needle through the first stitch again, but this time knitwise (from left to right; **Fig. 2**), pull the yarn through, then slip this stitch off the knitting needle.

Repeat from * for the desired number of stitches.

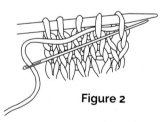

Figure 1

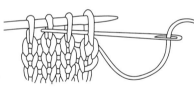

Figure 2

THREE-NEEDLE BIND-OFF

Place the stitches to be joined onto two separate needles and hold the needles parallel so that the two sides of knitting face together. Insert a third needle into the first stitch on each of two needles **(Fig. 1)** and knit them together as one stitch **(Fig. 2)**, *knit the next stitch on each needle the same way, then use the left needle tip to lift the first stitch over the second and off the needle **(Fig. 3)**. Repeat from * until no stitches remain on first two needles. Cut yarn and pull tail through last stitch to secure.

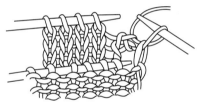

Figure 1

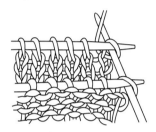

Figure 2

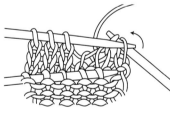

Figure 3

JENY'S SURPRISINGLY STRETCHY BIND-OFF

This aptly named bind-off is the brainchild of Jeny Staiman. The elasticity comes from a yarnover "collar" that is worked in conjunction with each stitch. When viewed straight on, the bind-off edge of the ribbing will have a hinged appearance at each transition between knit and purl stitches.

To Collar a Knit Stitch

Bring working yarn from back to front over needle in the opposite direction of a normal yarnover (yo) **(Fig. 1)**, knit the next stitch, then lift the yo over the top of the knitted stitch and off the needle **(Fig. 2)**.

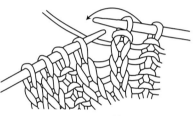

Figure 1

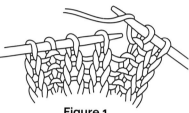

Figure 2

To Collar a Purl Stitch

Bring working yarn from front to back over needle as for a normal yarnover (yo) **(Fig. 3)**, purl the next stitch, then lift the yo over the top of the purled stitch and off the needle **(Fig. 4)**.

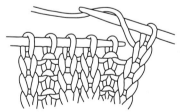

Figure 3

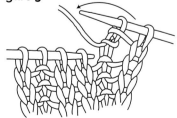

Figure 4

To begin, collar each of the first two stitches to match their knit or purl nature. Then pass the first collared stitch over the second and off the right needle—one stitch is bound off.

*Collar the next stitch according to its nature **(Fig. 5)**, then pass the previous stitch over the collared stitch and off the needle **(Fig. 6)**.

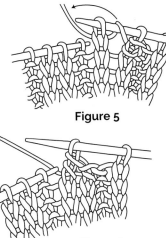

Figure 5

Figure 6

Repeat from * until one stitch remains on the right needle. Cut the yarn, leaving a 6" (15 cm) tail, then pull on the loop of the last stitch until the tail comes free.

Increases

BAR INCREASE

This type of increase forms a small bar similar to a purl stitch at the left-hand side of the increased stitch. Depending on the yarn and stitch pattern, this bar may or may not be noticeable.

Knitwise (K1F&B)

Knit into a stitch but leave the stitch on the left needle **(Fig. 1)**, then knit through the back loop of the same stitch **(Fig. 2)** and slip the original stitch off the needle **(Fig. 3)**.

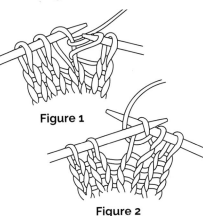

Figure 1

Figure 2

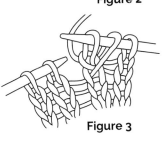

Figure 3

Purlwise (P1F&B)

You can work this increase purlwise by purling into the front and back of the same stitch.

LIFTED INCREASE (LI)

This type of increase is nearly invisible in the knitting. It can be worked to slant to the right or to the left, which can be used as a design element along raglan shaping. You can separate the increases by the desired number of stitches to form a prominent ridge.

Right Slant (RLI): Knit into the back of the stitch (in the "purl bump") in the row directly below the first stitch on the left needle **(Fig. 1)**, then knit the stitch on the needle **(Fig. 2)** and slip the original stitch off the needle.

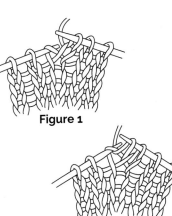

Figure 1

Figure 2

Left Slant (LLI): Knit the first stitch on the left needle, insert left needle tip into the back of the stitch (in the "purl bump") below the stitch just knitted **(Fig. 1)**, then knit this stitch **(Fig. 2)**.

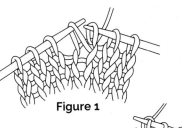

Figure 1

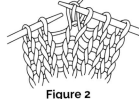

Figure 2

RAISED MAKE-ONE INCREASE (M1)

This type of increase is characterized by the tiny twisted stitch that forms at the base of the increase. Like the lifted method, it can slant to the right or the left, and you can separate the increases by the desired number of stitches to form a prominent ridge.

Right Slant (M1R): Use the left needle tip to lift the strand between the needle tips from back to front **(Fig. 1)**, then knit the lifted loop through the front to twist it **(Fig. 2)**.

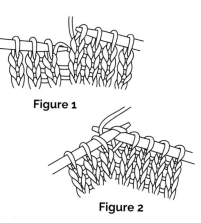

Figure 1

Figure 2

Left Slant (M1L): Use the left needle tip to lift the strand between the needle tips from front to back **(Fig. 1)**, then knit the lifted loop through the back to twist it **(Fig. 2)**.

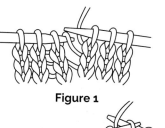

Figure 1

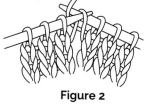

Figure 2

You can work these increases purlwise (M1P) by purling the lifted strand instead of knitting it.

Short-Rows

KNIT SIDE

Work to turning point, slip next stitch purlwise **(Fig. 1)**, bring the yarn to the front, then slip the same stitch back to the left needle **(Fig. 2)**, turn the work around and bring the yarn in position for the next stitch—one stitch has been wrapped, and the yarn is correctly positioned to work the next stitch. When you come to a wrapped stitch on a subsequent row, hide the wrap by working it together with the wrapped stitch as follows: Insert right needle tip under the wrap from the front **(Fig. 3)**, then into the stitch on the needle, and work the stitch and its wrap together as a single stitch.

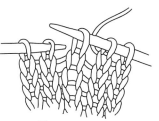

Figure 1

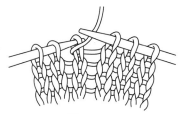

Figure 2

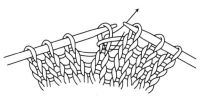

Figure 3

PURL SIDE

Work to the turning point, slip the next stitch purlwise to the right needle, bring the yarn to the back of the work **(Fig. 1)**, return the slipped stitch to the left needle, bring the yarn to the front between the needles **(Fig. 2)**, and turn the work so that the knit side is facing—one stitch has been wrapped, and the yarn is correctly positioned to knit the next stitch. To hide the wrap on a subsequent purl row, work to the wrapped stitch, use the tip of the right needle to pick up the wrap from the back, place it on the left needle **(Fig. 3)**, then purl it together with the wrapped stitch.

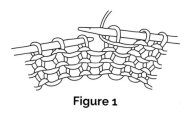

Figure 1

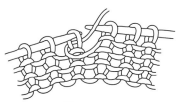

Figure 2

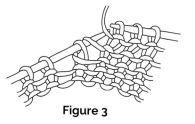

Figure 3

I-Cord

Using two double-pointed needles, cast on the desired number of stitches (usually three to five). *Without turning the needle, slide stitches to other end of needle, pull the yarn around the back, and knit the stitches as usual. Repeat from * for desired length.

Crochet Chain (ch)

Make a slipknot and place it on crochet hook if there isn't a loop already on the hook. *Yarn over hook and draw through loop on hook. Repeat from * for the desired number of stitches. To fasten off, cut yarn and draw end through last loop formed.

Grafting

KITCHENER STITCH

Arrange stitches on two needles so that there is the same number of stitches on each needle. Hold the needles parallel to each other with wrong sides of the knitting together. Allowing about ½" (1.3 cm) per stitch to be grafted, thread matching yarn on a tapestry needle. Work from right to left as follows:

1. Bring tapestry needle through the first stitch on the front needle as if to purl and leave the stitch on the needle **(Fig. 1)**.

2. Bring tapestry needle through the first stitch on the back needle as if to knit and leave that stitch on the needle **(Fig. 2)**.

3. Bring tapestry needle through the first front stitch as if to knit and slip this stitch off the needle, then bring tapestry needle through the next front stitch as if to purl and leave this stitch on the needle **(Fig. 3)**.

4. Bring tapestry needle through the first back stitch as if to purl and slip this stitch off the needle, then bring tapestry needle through the next back stitch as if to knit and leave this stitch on the needle **(Fig. 4)**.

Repeat Steps 3 and 4 until one stitch remains on each needle, adjusting the tension to match the rest of the knitting as you go. To finish, bring tapestry needle through the front stitch as if to knit and slip this stitch off the needle, then bring tapestry needle through the back stitch as if to purl and slip this stitch off the needle.

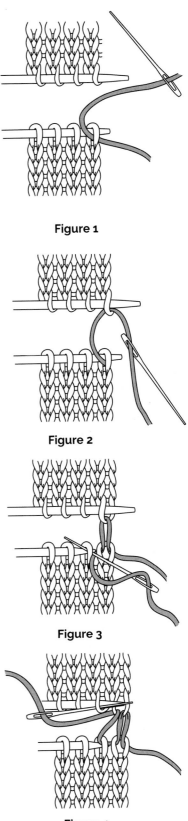

Figure 1

Figure 2

Figure 3

Figure 4

Sources for Yarns

**Alchemy Yarns
of Transformation**
P.O. Box 1080
Sebastopol, CA 95473
(707) 823-3276
alchemyyarns.com

Berroco
1 Tupperware Dr., Ste. 4
N, Smithfield, RI 02896
(401) 769-1212
berroco.com

Blue Moon Fiber Arts
56587 Mollenhour Rd.
Scappoose, OR 97056
(866) 802-9687
bluemoonfiberarts.com

BrooklynTweed
brooklyntweed.com

Classic Elite Yarns
16 Esquire Rd., Unit 2
North Billerica, MA 01862
(800) 343-0308
classiceliteyarns.com

Dragonfly Fibers
4104 Howard Ave.
Kensington, MD 20895
(301) 312-6883
dragonflyfibers.com

Dream in Color
dreamincoloryarn.com

Ella Rae/KFI
P.O. Box 336
315 Bayview Ave.
Amityville, NY 11701
knittingfever.com

Handmaiden Fine Yarn
handmaiden.ca

Hazel Knits
P.O. Box 28921
Seattle, WA 98118
hazelknits.com

Lorna's Laces
4229 N. Honore St.
Chicago, IL 60613
(773) 935-3803
lornaslaces.net

**Manos del Uruguay/
Fairmount Fibers, Ltd.**
P.O. Box 2082
Philadelphia, PA 19103
(888) 566-9970
fairmountfibers.com

**Miss Babs Hand-Dyed
Yarns & Fibers**
P.O. Box 78
Mountain City, TN 37683
(423) 727-0670
missbabs.com

Neighborhood Fiber Co.
neighborhoodfiberco.com

Quince & Co.
quinceandco.com

Rowan
Green Lane Mill
Holmfirth, West Yorkshire
England HD9 2DX
+44 (0)1484 681881
knitrowan.com
USA: Westminster Fibers
165 Ledge St.
Nashua, NH 03060
(800) 445-9276
westminsterfibers.com

**Schoppel Wolle/
Skacel Collection**
(800) 255-1278
skacelknitting.com

**Spud & Chloë/
Blue Sky Alpacas**
P.O. Box 88
Cedar, MN 55011
(888) 460-8862
spudandchloe.com

**String Theory
Colorworks**
25 Eastside Loop
Sandia Park, NM 87047
shop.selfstriping.com

Swans Island
231 Atlantic Hwy.
Northport, ME 04849
(888) 526-9526
swansislandcompany.com

SweetGeorgia Yarns
110-408 East Kent Ave. S.
Vancouver, BC
Canada V5X 2X7
(604) 569-6811
sweetgeorgiayarns.com

Tanis Fiber Arts
tanisfiberarts.com

Tilli Tomas
72 Woodland Rd.
Jamaica Plain, MA 02130
(617) 524-3330

The Uncommon Thread
Rodhus
16-30 Hollingdean Rd.
Brighton BN2 4AA
UK
theuncommonthread.co.uk

Wollmeise
Rohrspatz & Wollmeise
Schulstraße 10
85276 Pfaffenhofen
wollmeise-yarnshop.de

About the Designers

Susan B. Anderson has been knitting close to 30 years now. She is the author of *Topsy-Turvy Inside-Out Knit Toys* (Artisan, 2013), *Itty-Bitty Toys* (Artisan, 2013), *Spud & Chloë at the Farm* (Artisan, 2011), *Itty-Bitty Nursery* (Artisan, 2007), and *Itty-Bitty Hats* (Artisan, 2006). When Susan isn't working on books she teaches knitting workshops in all corners of the United States and beyond. Susan lives with her her four kids and husband in Madison, Wisconsin.

After working in various advertising agencies, **Thea Colman** took a break to be home with her young daughters and fell into knitwear design. She had always been a knitter who couldn't follow directions, so the idea of writing her own was pretty organic. Thea lives in the greater Boston area and blogs semi-regularly about both her designing and her cocktailing at **babycocktails.com.**

Sauniell Connally is a lover of all things fashion. Designing from a young age, Sauniell continues to study fashion, art, color, and texture to design clothing that complements women of every shape and size. Living in Brooklyn, New York, she spends her free time desperately trying to avoid fabric and yarn shops to keep her stash under control.

Joan Forgione's designs have been published in *Interweave Knits*, *Knit.1*, *Knit It*, *KnitSimple*, and *Vogue Knitting*, and featured in the books *60 More Quick Baby Knits* (Sixth & Spring, 2012) and *Knit.101* (Sixth & Spring, 2007). She has designed for Vijay Fibers, The Sanguine Gryphon, Knit Picks and ArtYarns. Her design portfolio can be viewed on Ravelry or by visiting **papermoonknits.com.**

A two-time national first place winner for the DAR American Heritage award for fiber arts, **Tanis Gray** has been knitting and designing for more than 25 years. A graduate of RISD, Tanis firmly believes that anyone can knit. With over 350 published knitting designs in books and magazines worldwide, Gray has worked at Martha Stewart, Vogue Knitting and Focus Features. Currently residing in Alexandria, Virginia with her husband, son, and lazy pug, she is working on her seventh knitting book for publication and is a regular guest on PBS's Knitting Daily TV. Read more of her writings and see her latest work at **tanisknits.com.**

Faina Goberstein is an accomplished knitwear designer, author, and a teacher. She teaches on craftsy.com, KnitLab, and other venues. Her designs can be found in *Interweave Knits*, *Vogue Knitting*, and various books and magazines. Faina is the co-author of *The Art of Seamless Knitting* (Interweave, 2013). Visit Faina's blog at **fainasknittingmode.blogspot.com.**

Melissa J. Goodale spends her days in Seattle dreaming up new designs and playing with yarn for her design company, Stick Chick Knits. Her projects expand to fill the space available; luckily, this doesn't seem to bother her loving husband and sons.

Marjan Hammink started to knit at the age of 4 when her grandmother observed: "You can write your name. Now I can teach you to knit." One of her first items was a small sock. Having grown up in a family where creativity was always taken seriously, she tries to always use good tools and superb fibers. She lives in the eastern, rural part of the Netherlands with husband, their 3 teenage sons, and two border terrier dogs.

Glenna Harris took up knitting as stress relief while studying for her Ph.D., then kept right on going. Her knitting and design philosophy is guided by a desire to constantly seek new challenges with interesting techniques and beautiful results through cables, colorwork, and more. Find her online at **crazyknittinglady.wordpress.com.**

Kelly Herdrich learned to knit while living in England, where she currently resides with her husband and three (not-yet-knitting) daughters. She formed kelly without a net designs in 2008 and is the designer of the popular In Threes: a Baby Cardigan.

Rosemary (Romi) Hill's work has appeared in numerous print and online publications, including *Interweave Knits*, *Knitscene*, and twistcollective.com. As part of a Ravelry group that set a goal of knitting 10 shawls in 2010, she got the crazy idea to design and knit 10 shawls. With 7 left to do, she started her first 7 Small Shawl eBook subscription collection. She has done two more since then and just embarked on a fourth.

Margaux Hufnagel has been published in *Interweave Knits*, *Knitscene*, and *Vogue Knitting*. She has taught classes at Patricia's Yarns in Hoboken, NJ and San Francisco's Atelier Yarns. She has numerous self-published patterns, including the popular *Fifth Avenue Infinity Scarf*. on her website: tentenknits.com. She currently lives and works in Massachusetts with her husband and son.

After nine years in Europe, **Susanna IC** now lives in San Antonio, Texas. She has an extensive background in studio arts and art history, which continue to inspire much of her knitting. Her work has appeared in numerous print publications, such as *Interweave Knits* and *Jane Austen Knits*, and online at twistcollective.com and knitty.com. Her projects and designs can be found on Ravelry and at **artqualia.com**.

Kirsten Kapur has been knitting, sewing, and creating for as long as she can remember. Her designs have been published in many books including *Knit to Flatter* (STC, 2014), *Knitting Architecture* (Interweave, 2013), *Knit Local* (Sixth&Spring, 2011), and many others. Kirsten lives in New York City with her husband and three children. Read her blog at **throughtheloops.typepad.com**.

Melissa LaBarre is a freelance knitwear designer and co-author of the books *Weekend Hats* (Interweave, 2011) and *New England Knits* (Interweave, 2010). Her designs have been published in *Knitscene*, *Vogue Knitting*, twistcollective.com, as well as design collections Quince & Co., Classic Elite, Valley Yarns, Blue Sky Alpacas, and BrooklynTweed, among many others. She lives in Massachusetts with her husband and small children. She blogs about knitting at **knittingschooldropout.com**.

Judy Marples's mother taught her to knit as a small child and she loved it right from the beginning. When she began creating her own designs she fell in love with the process and the challenge of design. Lace charts quickly took over her knitting life and she loves the logic of lace: the math involved and playing with graph paper and pencil. Read more about her on her blog **purlbumps.wordpress.com**.

Cirilia Rose lives in the Pacific Northwest and is the Brand Ambassador at Woolyarns. She spends her days tangled up in yarn and her evenings making messes in the kitchen. You can follow her fiber exploits at **ciriliarose.com**.

Erica Schlueter has been knitting for ages and has been teaching knitting for about half that time. She holds a BFA in fibers and studied both fashion and textile design. Erica's day job is her jewelry business Bent Metal that includes a line of pewter jewelry and stitch markers for knitters.

Åsa Söderman is the woman behind Åsa Tricosa. She knits with abandon in many parts of the world—not because she's in such high demand, but because she happens to move a lot. Her current obsession is with her own Ziggurat method, a technique for top-down, tailored, seamless, happy sweater making. You can find her online at **asatricosa.com**.

Carina Spencer is a Kansas City–based knitwear designer, personal chef, and mother who believes that liberal use of fine wool, cinnamon, and hugs will heal the world—or at least cozy the place up a bit.

Carol J. Sulcoski is a former attorney turned knitting designer, author, and hand-dyer. She is the author of *Sock Yarn Studio* (Lark, 2012) and *Knitting Socks With Handpainted Yarns* (Interweave, 2008), and is currently at work on two new books. Find her handpainted yarns and blog at **blackbunnyfibers.com**.

Carrie Sullivan, also known as Irish Girlie Knits, is a blogger and designer known for her deceptively simple, perfectly gorgeous designs such as Cotty and Summer Wind. Carrie also has designed for sock clubs and yarn companies such as Blue Moon Fiber Arts Rockin' Sock Club, the Woolgirl Sock Club, The Plucky Knitter Classics, and Kolläge Yarns. Her knitting adventures are blogged about at **wedonothaveaknittingproblem.blogspot.com**.

Ann Weaver has been designing handknits since 2007 while working a string of seemingly unrelated jobs. Her designs have been featured in *Brave New Knits* (Rodale, 2010), *Knitting Architecture* (Interweave, 2013), and many other books, as well as *Interweave Knits* and knitty.com. She is the author of four self-published design collections, including two based on Moby-Dick, her favorite novel. She currently lives in Baltimore.

Mindy Wilkes lives in suburban Cincinnati, Ohio. Her first love is small accessories. She loves designs that look complicated but are sweetly simple. When she's not knitting or designing, she's caring for her two small children. She also works and teaches knitting classes at her local yarn store. Her patterns can be found on Ravelry and in the pages of *Knitscene*, *Knit Now*, and various other print publications.

Heather Zoppetti lives in Lancaster, Pennsylvania with her husband and yarn collection. She can be found online at **hzoppettidesigns.com**.

Index

Knit something *for yourself . . .*
or to give *as a gift*

WITH THESE INSPIRING RESOURCES FROM INTERWEAVE

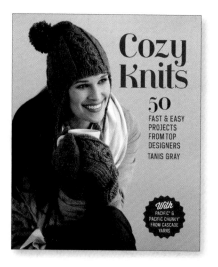

COZY KNITS
50 Fast & Easy Projects
from Top Designers

Tanis Gray

ISBN 978-1-62033-065-4, $18.95

KNITTING ARCHITECTURE
20 Patterns Exploring Form,
Function, and Detail

Tanis Gray

ISBN: 978-1-59668-780-6, $24.95

INTERWEAVE FAVORITES:
25 KNITTED ACCESSORIES
TO WEAR AND SHARE

Interweave

ISBN: 978-1-62033-826-1, $22.99

Available at your favorite retailer or  **knitting** daily **shop** *shop.knittingdaily.com*

knitting daily

Join Knittingdaily.com, an online community that shares your passion for knitting. You'll get a free e-newsletter, free patterns, a projects store, a daily blog, event updates, galleries, knitting tips and techniques, and more. Sign up at Knittingdaily.com.

INTERWEAVE
KNITS

From cover to cover, *Interweave Knits* magazine presents great projects for the beginner to the advanced knitter. Every issue is packed full of smart, captivating designs, step-by-step instructions, easy-to-understand illustrations, plus well-written, lively articles sure to inspire. Interweaveknits.com